# THE SERBIAN AMERICANS

# THE SERBIAN AMERICANS

Jerome Kisslinger

CHELSEA HOUSE PUBLISHERS

New York  Philadelphia

On the cover: Serbian-American girls in traditional dress.

**CHELSEA HOUSE PUBLISHERS**
Editor-in-Chief: Nancy Toff
Executive Editor: Remmel T. Nunn
Managing Editor: Karyn Gullen Browne
Copy Chief: Juliann Barbato
Picture Editor: Adrian G. Allen
Art Director: Maria Epes
Manufacturing Manager: Gerald Levine

**The Peoples of North America**
Senior Editor: Sean Dolan

**Staff for THE SERBIAN AMERICANS**
Associate Editor: Kate Barrett
Copy Editor: Mark Rifkin
Editorial Assistant: Gregory R. Rodríguez
Picture Researcher: PAR/NYC
Assistant Art Director: Loraine Machlin
Senior Designer: Noreen M. Lamb
Production Manager: Joseph Romano
Production Coordinator: Marie Claire Cebrián
Cover Illustration: Paul Biniasz
Banner Design: Hrana L. Janto

First Printing

1  3  5  7  9  8  6  4  2

**Library of Congress Cataloging-in-Publication Data**
Kisslinger, Jerome.
   The Serbian Americans / Jerome Kisslinger.
      p.   cm. — (Peoples of North America)
   Includes bibliographical references.
   Summary: Describes the history, culture, and religion of the Serbian Americans;
factors encouraging their emigration; and their acceptance as an ethnic group in North
America.
   ISBN 1-55546-133-6
        0-7910-0304-3 (pbk.)
   1. Serbian Americans—Juvenile literature.  [1. Serbian
Americans.]  I. Title.  II. Series.                              89-39123
E184.S5K57   1990                                               CIP
973'.0491822—dc20                                               AC

# CONTENTS

# THE PEOPLES OF NORTH AMERICA

CHELSEA HOUSE PUBLISHERS

# A NATION
# OF NATIONS

Daniel Patrick Moynihan

The Constitution of the United States begins: "We the People of the United States . . ." Yet, as we know, the United States is not made up of a single group of people. It is made up of many peoples. Immigrants from Europe, Asia, Africa, and Central and South America settled in North America seeking a new life filled with opportunities unavailable in their homeland. Coming from many nations, they forged one nation and made it their own. More than 100 years ago, Walt Whitman expressed this perception of America as a melting pot: "Here is not merely a nation, but a teeming Nation of nations."

Although the ingenuity and acts of courage of these immigrants, our ancestors, shaped the North American way of life, we sometimes take their contributions for granted. This fine series, *The Peoples of North America*, examines the experiences and contributions of the immigrants and how these contributions determined the future of the United States and Canada.

Immigrants did not abandon their ethnic traditions when they reached the shores of North America. Each ethnic group had its own customs and traditions, and each brought different experiences, accomplishments, skills, values, styles of dress, and tastes in food that lingered long after its arrival. Yet this profusion of differences created a singularity, or bond, among the immigrants.

The United States and Canada are unusual in this respect. Whereas religious and ethnic differences have sparked intolerance throughout the rest of the world—from the 17th-century religious wars to the 19th-century nationalist movements in Europe to the near extermination of the Jewish people under Nazi Germany—North Americans have struggled to learn how to respect each other's differences and live in harmony.

Millions of immigrants from scores of homelands brought diversity to our continent. In a mass migration, some 12 million immigrants passed through the waiting rooms of New York's Ellis Island; thousands more came to the West Coast. At first, these immigrants were welcomed because labor was needed to meet the demands of the Industrial Age. Soon, however, the new immigrants faced the prejudice of earlier immigrants who saw them as a burden on the economy. Legislation was passed to limit immigration. The Chinese Exclusion Act of 1882 was among the first laws closing the doors to the promise of America. The Japanese were also effectively excluded by this law. In 1924, Congress set immigration quotas on a country-by-country basis.

Such prejudices might have triggered war, as they did in Europe, but North Americans chose negotiation and compromise instead. This determination to resolve differences peacefully has been the hallmark of the peoples of North America.

The remarkable ability of Americans to live together as one people was seriously threatened by the issue of slavery. It was a symptom of growing intolerance in the world. Thousands of settlers from the British Isles had arrived in the colonies as indentured servants, agreeing to work for a specified number of years on farms or as apprentices in return for passage to America and room and board. When the first Africans arrived in the then-British colonies during the 17th century, some colonists thought that they too should be treated as indentured servants. Eventually, the question of whether the Africans should be viewed as indentured, like the English, or as slaves who could be owned for life, was considered in a Maryland court. The court's calamitous decree held that blacks were slaves bound to lifelong servitude, and so were their children. America went through a time of moral examination and civil war before it finally freed African slaves and their descendants. The principle that all people are created equal had faced its greatest challenge and survived.

Yet the court ruling that set blacks apart from other races fanned flames of discrimination that burned long after slavery was abolished—and that still flicker today. The concept of racism had existed for centuries in countries throughout the world. For instance, when the Manchus conquered China in the 13th century, they decreed that Chinese and Manchus could not intermarry. To impress their superiority on the conquered Chinese, the Manchus ordered all Chinese men to wear their hair in a long braid called a queue.

By the 19th century, some intellectuals took up the banner of racism, citing Charles Darwin. Darwin's scientific studies hypothesized that highly evolved animals were dominant over other animals. Some advocates of this theory applied it to humans, asserting that certain races were more highly evolved than others and thus were superior.

This philosophy served as the basis for a new form of discrimination, not only against nonwhite people but also against various ethnic groups. Asians faced harsh discrimination and were depicted by popular 19th-century newspaper cartoonists as depraved, degenerate, and deficient in intelligence. When the Irish flooded American cities to escape the famine in Ireland, the cartoonists caricatured the typical "Paddy" (a common term for Irish immigrants) as an apelike creature with jutting jaw and sloping forehead.

By the 20th century, racism and ethnic prejudice had given rise to virulent theories of a Northern European master race. When Adolf Hitler came to power in Germany in 1933, he popularized the notion of Aryan supremacy. *Aryan*, a term referring to the Indo-European races, was applied to so-called superior physical characteristics such as blond hair, blue eyes, and delicate facial features. Anyone with darker and heavier features was considered inferior. Buttressed by these theories, the German Nazi state from

1933 to 1945 set out to destroy European Jews, along with Poles, Russians, and other groups considered inferior. It nearly succeeded. Millions of these people were exterminated.

The tragedies brought on by ethnic and racial intolerance throughout the world demonstrate the importance of North America's efforts to create a society free of prejudice and inequality.

A relatively recent example of the New World's desire to resolve ethnic friction nonviolently is the solution the Canadians found to a conflict between two ethnic groups. A long-standing dispute as to whether Canadian culture was properly English or French resurfaced in the mid-1960s, dividing the peoples of the French-speaking Quebec Province from those of the English-speaking provinces. Relations grew tense, then bitter, then violent. The Royal Commission on Bilingualism and Biculturalism was established to study the growing crisis and to propose measures to ease the tensions. As a result of the commission's recommendations, all official documents and statements from the national government's capital at Ottawa are now issued in both French and English, and bilingual education is encouraged.

The year 1980 marked a coming of age for the United States's ethnic heritage. For the first time, the U.S. Census asked people about their ethnic background. Americans chose from more than 100 groups, including French Basque, Spanish Basque, French Canadian, Afro-American, Peruvian, Armenian, Chinese, and Japanese. The ethnic group with the largest response was English (49.6 million). More than 100 million Americans claimed ancestors from the British Isles, which includes England, Ireland, Wales, and Scotland. There were almost as many Germans (49.2 million) as English. The Irish-American population (40.2 million) was third, but the next largest ethnic group, the Afro-Americans, was a distant fourth (21 million). There was a sizable group of French ancestry (13 million), as well as of Italian (12 million). Poles, Dutch, Swedes, Norwegians, and Russians followed. These groups, and other smaller ones, represent the wondrous profusion of ethnic influences in North America.

Canada, too, has learned more about the diversity of its population. Studies conducted during the French/English conflict showed that Canadians were descended from Ukrainians, Germans, Italians, Chinese, Japanese, native Indians, and Eskimos, among others. Canada found it had no ethnic majority, although nearly half of its immigrant population had come from the British Isles. Canada, like the United States, is a land of immigrants for whom mutual tolerance is a matter of reason as well as principle.

The people of North America are the descendants of one of the greatest migrations in history. And that migration is not over. Koreans, Vietnamese, Nicaraguans, Cubans, and many others are heading for the shores of North America in large numbers. This mix of cultures shapes every aspect of our lives. To understand ourselves, we must know something about our diverse ethnic ancestry. Nothing so defines the North American nations as the motto on the Great Seal of the United States: *E Pluribus Unum*— Out of Many, One.

# SERBIAN AND AMERICAN

Most Americans, if they know anything about Serbia at all, are vaguely aware of it as a small land in Eastern Europe whose complex politics and history somehow implicated it in the outbreak of World War I. More well informed individuals might know that it is the largest and most populous of the 6 constituent republics of Yugoslavia, a nation that is home to 20 different nationalities, 3 official languages, 2 alphabets, and 3 major religions. But few know that there are dozens of Serbian communities across the continent of North America and that today there are more than 250,000 Serbian Americans living in the United States and Canada. This number encompasses those who have arrived recently in search of economic opportunity, political refugees who have fled Yugoslavia in the years since World War II as well as the descendants of the Serbian immigrants who came to North America between 1880 and 1914, during the second great wave of European immigration. Still other Serbian Americans can trace their beginnings in the New World to the pioneers, the generation of adventurers who first made their way to the new nation of the United States in the first half of the 19th century. Together, these individuals constitute a proud and diverse community, one that celebrates both its roots in the homeland and its place in American society.

The homeland of the Serbian Americans is a mountainous inland region of the Balkan Peninsula, bordered by Hungary on the north and Bulgaria and Romania on the east. It is Yugoslavia's easternmost region; Europe's second longest river, the Danube, flows through it. In past centuries, Serbia has known both freedom and subjugation; it has existed as an independent nation and has been ruled by Turkey and Austria-Hungary. In the modern era, Serbian nationalists have continued to press for greater autonomy. Religion and language remain the most crucial elements of the Serbian national identity. For more than 700 years, most Serbs have been members of the Eastern Orthodox church. They share a language with another South Slavic people, the Croatians, but the Serbs use a modified version of the Cyrillic alphabet; the Croatians, who are predominantly Roman Catholic, use the Roman alphabet.

Some Serbs claim that the first of their ancestors to immigrate to the New World was a member of the crew of Columbus's fleet, but the first Serbs whose presence in America can be documented did not arrive until the 1830s and 1840s. These individuals came not from the homeland itself but from Serbian settlements scattered throughout the Austro-Hungarian territories surrounding Serbia, especially those found on the Dalmatian coast of the Adriatic Sea.

Since many of the early immigrants had been farmers, fishermen, or sailors, it is not surprising that they gravitated toward the coastal regions of the United States—first to New Orleans, Louisiana, and Galveston, Texas, and then on to California. Serbs in the San Francisco area helped settle the gold and silver mining towns of California, Nevada, and Utah. The earliest pioneer communities were fragile outposts on a large and alien continent in which Serbs lived together with Croatians, Russians, and other Slavs. Within a short time, however, with the great influx of Serbian immi-

grants that began in the 1880s, Serbs began to form their own distinct communities.

These new arrivals, known as old settlers, came to the New World between approximately 1880 and the outbreak of World War I as part of the massive migration from southern and eastern Europe often referred to as the second great wave of European immigration. (The first great wave peaked in the 1840s and consisted mostly of immigrants from western and northern Europe: English, Germans, Irish, Swedes, and others.) During the second great wave, millions of Italians, Jews, Slavs, and other eastern and southern Europeans emigrated to America to escape intolerable political constraints and devastating economic conditions.

Like the pioneers, the old settlers came almost entirely from Austro-Hungarian territories adjacent to Serbia itself. They found new homes, almost without exception, in the northeastern and central regions of the United States and Canada, the center of the continent's heavy industry. To this day, the largest and most active Serbian communities can be found within commuting distance of a mine or factory, in such towns as Lackawanna, New York; Steelton, Pennsylvania; and Windsor, Ontario.

*The monastery of the patriarchate of Peć dates from the 13th century and is renowned for its beautiful frescoes. The Serbians' Orthodox faith is perhaps the most important component of their national identity.*

The Serbian population of North America swelled significantly once again after World War II, when tens of thousands of refugees fled their battered homeland. Most of these émigrés were opponents of Yugoslavia's postwar government, which was led by the Communist Josip Broz Tito. Unlike the earlier immigrants, most of whom tended to be unskilled and uneducated, many of the newcomers were highly educated and had been professionals and members of the middle and upper class in Yugoslavia. Many had trouble adapting to the abrupt loss of their homeland and the comparative lack of opportunities available to them here. They tended to settle in or near established Serbian communities, to which they brought new vitality.

The most recent wave of Serbian immigration has taken place since 1965. Most of these immigrants have come to the United States and Canada in search of economic opportunity. Like the newcomers, many of the recent arrivals are doctors, engineers, or scholars. Because both the United States and Yugoslavia have opened their borders, many recent arrivals move freely back and forth across the Atlantic. Unhampered by political restrictions, they often plan to return to Yugoslavia permanently at some point and tend to remain isolated from the longer-established Serbian-American community.

*Young Yugoslavian performers in traditional costumes banter with each other offstage after a recital at a high school in Buffalo, New York. Serbian-American cultural organizations often sponsor such performances.*

While the members of each of these groups might disagree on what it means to be Serbian, it is undeniable that they share a collective ethnic identity. For most, this identity is maintained through belonging to a Serbian Orthodox church. In recent years, hundreds of Serbs across the United States and Canada have donated generously to the construction of the neglected St. Vraćar Cathedral in Belgrade. For them, being Serbian, or *srpstvo*, means retaining close ties to the traditions of the church. For others, it entails participation in music and folklore groups that celebrate the culture of the homeland. And some would argue that there is no better way to capture the essence of Serbia than through a succulent meal of roast peppers, lamb and cabbage, and plum brandy.

To a degree, Serbian Americans are further bound together through an awareness of a long and turbulent common history that embraces not only the homeland's past—Serbia's golden age under the Nemanjic dynasty in the 13th and 14th centuries, the fall of Serbia to the Turks at Kosovo in 1389, the years of Ottoman and Hapsburg domination, the Serbian struggle for independence, and its present-day role as an autonomous republic within Yugoslavia—but also the legacy of more than 150 years in North America: from the Louisiana oyster fisherman of the 1830s and the California innkeeper of the 1850s to the Pittsburgh steelworker of 1910, the political refugee of the 1950s, and the engineer of today. They are proud not only of their homeland's long struggle to resist domination by foreign powers but of the traditions and customs that have survived the passage to North America.

Serbian Americans exult as well in the myriad contributions of individual Serbians to American life. Through the achievements of such prominent figures as inventor Nikola Tesla, actor John Malkovich, basketball great Pete Maravich, and the often unrecognized efforts of the Serbian immigrants who mined this continent's coal, manned its mills and factories, and made a better life for themselves and their families, Serbians have proved themselves to be more than a colorful fringe on our social fabric—they are woven into its very fiber.

# THE HOMELAND IN HISTORY

The ancestors of today's Serbs were Slavic tribesmen who first appeared on the Balkan Peninsula almost 1,600 years ago. Like the Goths, Vandals, Franks, and other groups, they raided and then settled the weakened outskirts of the declining Roman Empire. The Slavs migrated southwest into the Balkans from their original home near the Carpathian mountains, arriving in the late 4th or 5th century A.D., and had already been in the region for 1,000 years when Columbus landed in the New World.

These Slavic tribesmen were not the first to inhabit the Balkan Peninsula. Stone Age artifacts from the region indicate that its original settlers were the Illyrians, who were later joined by the Thracians and, in the 4th century B.C., by Celtic groups. The Romans moved into the Balkans in the 3rd century B.C.; Moesia was their name for the province that contained what is now modern Serbia. In many of the major cities in today's Yugoslavia, traces of the Roman period are still evident. At Split, in Croatia, there are ruins of an extensive Roman city built in and around the palace of the emperor Diocletian on the coast of the Adriatic Sea. In what is called the old town of Split, narrow, winding streets encircle the teeming marketplace crowded

within the walls of Diocletian's palace, and a cathedral rises from the site of what once was his mausoleum.

Over the centuries, the Slavs, a primarily agricultural people, mixed with the original inhabitants and later invaders of the Balkan Peninsula and developed the distinct characteristics that would later be defined as Serbian, the most important of which is the Serbo-Croatian language. Slavs elsewhere on the peninsula and across Europe were undergoing a similar process, so that although all Slavs are united by a common ancestry and by their speaking related languages, they are also divided into subgroups and national and ethnic groups. The West Slavs are the Poles, Czechs, and Slovaks; the South Slavs are the Serbs, Croats, Slovenes, Macedonians, and Bulgars; and the East Slavs are the Russians, Ukrainians, and Belorussians. Their languages all have certain elements in common, although the Slavs use two different alphabets.

## Rough Terrain

Serbia's location and rugged landscape played a critical factor in its historical development. The Julian Alps in the northwest corner of the peninsula and the Dinaric Alps along the Adriatic coast helped isolate Serbia from western Europe. The Croatians, who settled the area west of Serbia and with whom the Serbs share their language, were allied early in their history with Rome by virtue of their conversion to Roman Catholicism, and they conducted trade and fought frequent wars with Venice, then a powerful military and commercial power. By contrast, Serbia's location and topography virtually ensured that its greatest influences would come from the East. Hungary has been described as the "doormat of Europe," where the Eastern powers wipe their boots before entering, but often their route of conquest led through Serbia first, and until the 20th century the greatest threats to Serbian autonomy came from that direction.

## The Struggle for the Serbian Soul

When emperor Diocletian divided the great empire, the line of division cut through Serbia. Centuries later, with the secular power of the remnants of the Roman Empire waning at the besieged Eastern capital of Constantinople, its spiritual successors waged a struggle for the souls of the Slavs. Like most of the South and East Slavs (except for the Croats and the Slovenes), the Serbs were converted to the Eastern Orthodox branch of Catholicism, rather than to the Roman church, sometime around the 9th century, probably as a result of the work of the "Apostles to the Slavs," Saints Cyril and Methodius, and their disciples Clement and Naum. The most significant difference, from the standpoint of the Serbs, was that their allegiance to Eastern Orthodoxy meant that they would look toward Constantinople, not Rome, for spiritual authority and that the mass and other church services were sung in the Slavic tongue of Old High Slavonic rather than in Latin.

*This illustration of a scribe at his lectern is found in the the most celebrated of medieval Serbian manuscripts, the Gospel Book of Prince Miroslav, which dates from approximately 1180. The illuminated manuscript is believed to be the work of the scribe Gligorija, who served in the court of Miroslav, prince of Hum, a brother of Stefan Nemanja.*

*A 15th-century wooden icon of Saint Sava (left) and Saint Simeon. The son of Stefan Nemanja, Saint Sava is revered as the patron saint of the Serbian Orthodox church, the first bishop of Serbia, and as the catalyst of a cultural renaissance that included the beginnings of Serbian literature.*

Serbia was formally tied to the Eastern Orthodox church between 1170 and 1196, during the reign of Stefan Nemanja, its first great ruler. For the previous 400 years, the Serbs had been ruled by *župans*, feudal lords who controlled limited areas with their own armies while nominally swearing allegiance to the Bulgarian or Byzantine Empire. Although many prominent župans before Stefan Nemanja had fought against outside domination by the Byzantines and others, the Nemanjic dynasty was the first to achieve full independence. It ruled over Serbia for the next 200 years.

In 1196, Stefan Nemanja stepped down as grand župan and retired to Mount Athos in Greece, a spiritual center of the Byzantine church, where he and his son Rastko founded the first Serbian monastery. In 1219, Rastko, who would later be canonized as Saint Sava, was named the first bishop of the Serbian Orthodox church by the Byzantine patriarch. Two years earlier, Saint Sava's older brother, Stefan, had been crowned the first king of Serbia. Serbia was now solidly established as an autonomous nation firmly allied with the Eastern church even though it was Rome that crowned the king. Sava and Stefan were also responsible for the first original work of literature in Serbian, a biography of their father, Stefan Nemanja.

## The Golden Age

Although surrounded by frequently hostile neighbors and troubled by internal dissension, Serbia flourished under Nemanjic rule. The dynasty reached its peak between 1331 and 1355 under the rule of Czar Stefan

*A detail from the early-14th-century fresco* King Milutin as Donor, *from the King's Church in Studenica. Also known as Stephen Uroš II, Milutin became vastly wealthy by developing Serbia's silver mines, and he vowed to build one church for every year of his reign.*

*Detail from the late-13th-century fresco* The Dormition of the Virgin, *which appears on the west wall of the nave of the Church of Sopoćani. Religious art flourished under Nemanjic rule, a period recalled now as Serbia's golden age.*

Dušan, who extended Serbia's frontiers to the Sava and Danube rivers to the north, in lands previously held by Hungary, and to the Gulf of Corinth in the south, conquering former Byzantine holdings in what are now Albania, Bulgaria, and Greece. Dušan also developed one of the first legal codes in Europe, a complex combination of Byzantine legal traditions and Serbian customs, and he imported experts from western Europe to help develop Serbia's mining centers. Monasteries, particularly in Kosovo, flourished as centers of Orthodox learning, and with the establishment of an independent patriarchate at Peć, the church gained even greater autonomy. The architecture of the monasteries and the beautiful frescoes contained within remain eloquent testaments to the faith and artistic achievement of Serbia's golden age.

## Five Hundred Years Under the Turks

Serbia entered a period of decline with the death of Dušan in 1355. His successors failed to control the local feudal lords, who acted as kings within their limited realm, and the forces of the Ottoman Empire relentlessly carved away at Serbia's holdings. Within a little more than a century after Dušan's death, with the fall of its last fortress to the Turks in 1459, Serbia had lost virtually its final remnant of autonomy. Its most symbolic defeat came only 34 years after the death of its greatest king. On June 28, 1389, Serbian forces under Czar Lazar were defeated by the troops of the Turkish prince Murad I at the Battle of Kosovo. Both leaders were killed, and both armies were devastated. Although the Ottomans won, unrest in other regions of their empire prevented them from immediately pursuing their advantage. Serbian princes managed to maintain some degree of sovereignty for the next 70 years, and the Serbs continued to assert their national identity by building magnificent monasteries decorated with statues and frescoes.

Over time, the Turks solidified their control over Serbia. The Turkish ruler, known as the sultan, dispatched governors and officials to Serbia to see to the business of administration. Heavy taxes were imposed, and Serbian children were impressed for training to become Janissaries, members of the elite fighting corps of the Ottoman military. The peasantry, the largest class in medieval Serbian society, was made to work for Turkish overlords on estates known as *timars*.

Although the Ottomans were Muslims, they allowed the Serbians to continue to practice Christianity. Through a system known as *millet*, the Ottomans gave local religious leaders the authority to maintain order and collect taxes. This system not only allowed churches and monasteries to function over centuries of Turkish rule but actually invested religious leaders with greater power than they had theretofore wielded. Over time, however, the Turks came to rely on officials of the Greek Orthodox church to control the independent-minded Serbs, who greatly resented the interference of the Greeks. This domination enhanced the status of the Serbian village priest as a defender of Serbian identity and freedom.

Despite its relatively tolerant beginnings, Ottoman rule grew increasingly harsh, particularly as the empire began to fragment under the force of internal pressures. In the late 18th and 19th centuries, atrocities committed by the Ottomans against their subjects on the Balkan Peninsula elicited the outrage of the rest of Europe. Driven by fear and poverty, large numbers of Serbs fled the homeland to resettle in lands controlled by Austria-Hungary. Many of them settled in a military frontier zone that had been established in the 16th century by the Hapsburg monarchs as a buffer against the Ottomans. These frontiersmen, or *Granicari*, pledged military service in exchange for land rights and political and religious freedom. Many settled in a region called the Vojvodina, a flat plain between Serbia and Hungary. Others went to Lika, a rocky province of Croatia, or to other remote areas of Croatia and Dalmatia. In time, deteriorating conditions would drive the descendants of these *precani* ("over the river") Serbs to emigrate to the New World.

*The Great Serbian Migration, an 1896 painting by Paja Jovanovic, depicts the flight of approximately 36,000 families in 1690 from the Turkish-controlled area of South Serbia into the autonomous regions north of the Sava and Danube rivers.*

The Ottoman occupation had a profound effect on the development of Serbian culture. Under the Turks, Serbia remained isolated from western Europe, cut off to a great extent from the enormous cultural and technological developments that arose from the Renaissance, the Enlightenment, and the scientific revolution. The Ottomans had little interest in any aspect of the Serbian economy other than agriculture, which meant there was virtually no industrial development, and the populace suffered under the burden of exorbitant taxation and the privations engendered by virtually unceasing warfare. Anthropologist Joel Halpern describes how deeply the Ottoman occupation has affected the Serbian self-image to this day:

> It is impossible to converse with a Serbian peasant without having him mention the *pet stotia godina pod Turcima* (500 years under the Turks)—whether as a reason for the low standard of living, a comment on national history, or an excuse for a neighbor's behavior.

## Struggling for Freedom

Ottoman rule did not go unchallenged in Serbia, although the most significant resistance was usually posed by other outsiders eager to gain influence in the Balkans—most often Austria, Hungary, and Russia. The exact geographic extent of Turkish control on the peninsula varied according to its ability to resist these challengers. The Vojvodina, for example, sometimes rested under Austro-Hungarian control, sometimes under Turkish suzerainty.

Under the rule of Catherine the Great, Russia assumed the role of the liberator of the Slavs and Orthodox Christians who were under the sway of the Ottoman Empire. Serbs fought with a joint Russian and Austrian force that defeated the Ottomans in the early 1790s; this victory set the stage for Serbian independence. The erosion of the central authority of the sultan freed the Janissaries to act independently in Serbia, and the result was a period of lawlessness, rapacity, and cruel excess. After the murder of several

*Karadjordje Petrovic, or Black George, the former pig merchant who led the first of Serbia's many rebellions against Turkish rule.*

prominent Serbs by the Janissaries went without redress by the sultan, the livestock merchant Karadjordje (Black George) Petrovic organized a revolt. His forces drove the Turks from Belgrade in 1805, and over the next seven years Karadjordje sought to establish an effective government, calling the first Council of Notables, creating a Senate modeled on the Western democracies, and beginning administrative and educational reforms. With Austria unwilling to guarantee assistance, Karadjordje allied Serbia with Russia, receiving in return the first recognition of its autonomy. But by 1813, with its protector occupied in defending itself against the Grande Armée of Napoléon Bonaparte, Serbia found itself again vulnerable to Turkish invasion. Karadjordje was put to flight by October. The new Turkish administration reenacted the worst excesses of the previous regime, with the culmination occurring in December 1814, when 200 of Serbia's leading citizens were beheaded or impaled.

Many of those Serbian leaders who avoided the massacre fled across the border to the Vojvodina, whose monasteries at Fruska Gora had become a stronghold of Serbian nationalism. Led by Miloš Obrenović, the revived Serbian resistance defeated the Turks, with Obrenović receiving guarantees of conditional autonomy and his family's hereditary right to the position of Vrhovni Knez, or supreme chief, in exchange for, among other conditions, arranging the assassination of Karadjordje, who had returned from exile and with his followers was clamoring for complete independence.

With the resurgence in national pride that accompanied Serbia's fight for independence came a renewed interest in the land's native culture. Before this period, literature was tied closely to the church and was written exclusively in Old High Slavonic, not the Serbo-Croatian tongue spoken by the majority of the populace. The uprisings against the Turks and Serbia's attempts to establish a representative government stimulated interest in literature and other art forms that would more accurately reflect the everyday life of the people. In the 19th century, Vuk Karadzić pub-

*Vuk Karadzić, whose collections of folklore and linguistic reforms paved the way for the use of Serbian as a literary language.*

lished vast collections of Serbo-Croatian folklore and poetry, including lyric poems sung at work or to accompany dancing and epics recalling heroic feats in battles from Serbia's past. Karadzić also championed linguistic reforms that provided Serbians with a literary language based on the vernacular, or the spoken word. In this way, books moved from the domain of a small, elite segment of Serbia to become, for the first time, the authentic voice of the Serbian people. This transition opened the way for many innovations in Serbian poetry and drama, and it was in this shift from a church-centered writing to the language and concerns of the common people that the first Serbian novels were born.

*An engraving of a riotous election-day scene in Serbia in the late 19th century. After 500 years of domination by the Turks, the transition to self-rule was not always smooth.*

The remaining years of the 19th century proved extremely tumultuous for Serbia as it struggled to establish itself as an independent nation despite its low level of economic development, frequent political turmoil, and the often unwelcome attention of its meddlesome and more powerful neighbors. Within Serbia, the descendants of Karadjordje and Obrenović vied for power, as did those advocating a constitutional monarchy and those favoring autocratic one-man rule. The ruler and form of government changed many times; Serbia became a monarchy in 1882 and a constitutional monarchy in 1903.

Serbia's success in throwing off Turkish rule and maintaining autonomy made it the likely champion of Balkan and South Slav nationalism, a role it embraced. When the member nations of the Balkan League (Serbia, Montenegro, Greece, and Bulgaria) went to war with the Ottoman Empire in 1912 in order to liberate its remaining European possessions, Serbia emerged as the strongest Balkan state, having succeeded not only in defeating the Ottomans but in taking Macedonia from Bulgaria.

Throughout this period, Austria-Hungary had cast a wary eye on the nationalist upheaval in the Balkans, well aware that the insistence on self-determination was liable to make the Slavic nationalities within its empire that much more difficult to govern. Tensions between Serbia and Austria-Hungary peaked in June 1914 when Archduke Franz Ferdinand, the heir to the Austrian throne, was assassinated while visiting the city of Sarajevo, Bosnia. The culprits were Bosnian Serbs seeking independence for Bosnia, but the Austrians accused the Serbian government of complicity in the deed and issued an ultimatum concerning the investigation of the slaying that, had Serbia complied, would have severely compromised its hard-won sovereignty. War between Serbia and Austria-Hungary was the immediate result, with the complex system of treaties and alliances that bound the major European powers soon embroiling them as well.

## The Price of Unity

World War I shattered both the Hapsburg and Ottoman empires, leaving the South Slavs to determine their future political organization. In 1918 a union of the South Slavs was announced, in the form of the Kingdom of the Serbs, Croats, and Slovenes. The new nation included the other South Slav inhabitants of the Balkan Peninsula—the Bosnians, Macedonians, and Montenegrins—as well as other national minorities. From the outset, it was burdened with difficulties. Accustomed to their own independence, the Serbs favored a strong central government in which they would play the leading role; other groups feared Serbian dominance as a threat to their own autonomy. The kingdom's first decade was plagued by struggles between the Serbs and Croatian nationalists, which climaxed in 1928 with the murder of Croatian leaders in the national assembly.

In an attempt to impose order, King Alexander dissolved Parliament, established a royal dictatorship, and changed the name of his nation to Yugoslavia (land of the South Slavs) in 1929, but nationalist unrest continued. Alexander was assassinated by Croat terrorists in 1934; ensuing governments flirted with the Fascist nations of Germany and Italy in order to placate the growing right-wing movement (led by the Croat Fascist party, the Ustaše) in Yugoslavia. Following the outbreak of World War II in 1939, Yugoslavia sought to remain on good terms with Germany without surrendering its sovereignty, but the Nazis responded by invading on April 6, 1941. Decades of dissension had left the nation ill prepared to defend itself; Yugoslavia capitulated 11 days later.

The Nazis established puppet regimes in both Serbia and Croatia. In Croatia, the Ustaše government, headed by Ante Pavelić, set out to "purify" the area of its substantial Serbian population: One-third were

*Accompanied by his black-clad mother, Queen Marie, the boy king, Peter II, marches in the funeral procession of his father, King Alexander of Yugoslavia, who was assassinated by Croatian terrorists in 1934. The kingdom of the South Slavs was plagued by internal dissension.*

be shot, one-third deported, and the remaining third converted to Roman Catholicism. Hundreds of thousands of Serbs were murdered; later in the war, the Serbs retaliated by massacring Croats.

## Tito

Yugoslavia was saved by an active resistance movement. The most important resistance group was the Partisans, led by the Croatian Communist Josip Broz Tito. Beginning in the late 1930s, Tito had called upon Croats and Serbs to put aside their differences and band together in a united front to combat fascism, which he saw as the greatest threat to Yugoslavia's future. Yugoslavians of all ethnic groups served in the Partisans. The other leading resistance group, the Četniks, were primarily Serbian; they were led by Colonel Draža Mihajlović, a former officer in the Royal Yugoslav Army. Cooperation between the two groups was minimal, and they often fought each other in addition to the Nazis. By 1943, Tito had the upper hand in his struggle with both; by the following year the Nazis were on the run, and the Partisans were receiving assistance from the Allies. Tito's government began setting up local government councils in liberated territories during the war, so that when the Nazis surrendered in April 1945, the Communists were able to take control of postwar Yugoslavia.

Under Tito, Serbia became one of six federal republics in the reconstituted Yugoslavia. The constitution of 1946 divided Serbia by creating the autonomous provinces of Kosovo and Vojvodina. Tito held power in Yugoslavia until his death in 1980, guiding it from a close alliance with the Soviet Union to a position of leadership among the nonaligned nations of the world while maintaining the Communist economic system of collective ownership.

Since Tito's death, economic problems and an upsurge in ethnic nationalism have threatened the unity he helped create. Yugoslavia is burdened by a huge trade deficit, foreign debt, an almost 300 percent inflation rate, and growing unemployment, difficulties exacerbated by the nation's decentralized economic and

*Prince Paul, seen here with Adolf Hitler, was one of the three regents to rule on behalf of the young King Peter between 1935 and 1941. Although his sympathies in the developing European crisis lay with Great Britain and its allies, he was unsuccessful in his efforts to preserve a neutral stance in response to Nazi pressure.*

political system, which leaves much power to the republics. Strife between the nation's ethnic groups, long a problem, grew more severe in the late 1980s, particularly in the autonomous province of Kosovo, where the Albanian majority has long been demanding increased political and economic power. Albanian aspirations have collided with the wishes of the Serbs, who fear for the rights of the Serbian minority in Kosovo, which, as the seat of the medieval kingdom and patriarchate and the site of the great 1389 battle against the Turks, they view as the symbolic center of their national identity. In 1989, Serbs demonstrated against the unrest in Kosovo and for constitutional reforms

*Marshal Josip Broz Tito, leader of the Partisan guerrilla forces during World War II and then head of the government of Yugoslavia until his death in 1980.*

*In the years since Tito's death, ethnic strife has divided Yugoslavia. Seen here is Serbian president Slobodan Milosevic, a fiery proponent of Serbian nationalism, giving a speech in Belgrade in February 1989 in which he announced the arrest of Albanian demonstrators in Kosovo.*

aimed at securing direct Serbian control of the police and other enforcement agencies. Under the direction of Slobodan Milosevic, head of the Serbian party, Serbs have also continued to press for political change leading to greater autonomy.

It is perhaps inevitable that a summary of Serbian history end on a note of discord. Serbia has lived for centuries in the midst of turmoil. It has suffered occupation and oppression at the hands of foreign empires, and it has survived war and revolution. Now it must endure the conflicts between centralization and nationalism as multiethnic Yugoslavia attempts to reform its economic and political structure. Over the past 100 years or so each of these upheavals has generated a new wave of immigration to North America.

# PIONEERS AND OLD SETTLERS

Every immigrant has his or her story. Behind the statistics and generalizations are individual human beings, each of whom had to make the difficult choice to leave behind family and home. Nevertheless, it is possible to divide the history of Serbian immigration into four distinct groups: the pioneers, the old settlers, the newcomers, and the recent arrivals. Each group had its own reasons for coming, and each has left its distinctive mark on the Serbian-American community and on North America as a whole.

## The Pioneers

The pioneer Serbs arrived in the first eight decades of the 19th century. Like the early Croatian immigrants who came at about this same time, almost all were young men, and many were sailors or fishermen who came from small villages along the Dalmatian coast. They established sizable Serbian communities in the port cities of New Orleans, Galveston, and later, in San Francisco, where they found climates similar to what they had known in the homeland and were able to find jobs in the fishing and shipping industries.

Whereas many worked the oyster beds in the Gulf of Mexico, the more adventurous followed the gold rush to California and the remote regions of Nevada, Utah, and Colorado.

While only a few immigrants struck it rich as prospectors, many Serbians remained in California and the West, where they settled into more stable careers as merchants, restaurant owners, and produce farmers. Indeed, the Serbians (and the Croatians) were so successful at farming that the Pajaro Valley of California came to be called "Little Dalmatia," and Olga Markovich, a well-known writer on Serbs in North America, reported that one pioneer grape farmer in the Fresno area used the brand name Serbian Blue for his popular product.

Because the origins, settlement patterns, and last names of early Serbian settlers are often indistinguishable from those of other South Slav immigrants, the study of pioneer and old-settler communities is often difficult. The earliest South Slav immigrant organizations in New Orleans and California used the umbrella term *Slavonic* to refer to both their Serbian and Croatian members. Until World War I, immigration and census statistics added to the confusion by listing immigrants according to their country of origin rather than their ethnicity, thereby classifying Serbs as Austro-Hungarians or Turks or else lumping them together with the Bulgarians. Only early church records help more accurately classify the South Slavs because they enable the researcher to distinguish Orthodox Serbian worshipers from Roman Catholic and Muslim South Slavs.

Whether Croatian or Serb, these Slavonic pioneers tended to be adventurers who came to the new continent more in search of a quick, temporary change of fortune than a permanent home. Frustrated by limited opportunities in the old country, they were guided by a restless spirit suited to the frontiers they settled— none more so than one George Fisher.

Fisher received his American name from bystanders who watched him jump ship at the mouth of the Delaware River. He swam ashore to escape from his

redemptioner pledge, which obliged him to pay for his passage by becoming a bond servant upon his arrival in the New World. Fisher's given name is more convincingly Serbian: He was christened Djordje Šagic in 1795 in a Serbian settlement in western Hungary. Politically minded and venturesome from an early age, he took part in the Karadjordje rebellion. When the Turks temporarily prevailed, Šagic took passage for the United States, arriving in Philadelphia in September 1815.

Though Fisher became an American citizen early on, he continued to wander, from Pennsylvania to Mississippi to Mexico and then on to Texas, where, perhaps hearing an echo of Serbia's struggle in Texas's battle for independence from Mexico, he fought enthusiastically for the Lone Star Republic. He published a liberal Spanish-language paper, helped to organize the first supreme court of the republic, and held a number of positions in state government after Texas joined the United States.

Like many of his fellow Serbs, Fisher felt the lure of California. After a brief journey to Panama in 1851, he ventured to San Francisco, where he served the new state of California as secretary of the land commission, justice of the peace, and county judge. In the last three years of his life he also served as consul for Greece.

Although not all pioneers achieved the prominence of Fisher, many shared his restless energy and determination, but by the 1880s the character of the North American economy had changed, as had the nature of the immigrants who were arriving on its shores in greater numbers than ever before. No less courageous or persistent than those of Fisher's generation, the new wave of Serbian immigrants sought opportunity not in America's wild western territories but in its industrial heartland.

## Old Settlers

The next wave of Serbs to cross the Atlantic were part of the greatest mass migration in history. Between 1880 and 1914, approximately 20 million Europeans arrived in North America, most of them of southern or eastern European origin. These Slavs, Hungarians, Jews, Italians, and Greeks looked and sounded very foreign to their northern European predecessors. This was the era memorialized by the Statue of Liberty and the sonnet "The New Colossus," by Emma Lazarus, which is inscribed on its pedestal. Lazarus refers to this wave of poor, uneducated immigrants of dark complexion as the "wretched refuse" of Europe's "teeming shore"; the "huddled masses yearning to breathe free."

Though political freedom was a motive for some, economic opportunity was likely the primary motivation for most of the huddled masses of the great wave. Many who came were sojourners, travelers who

planned to settle only long enough to amass sufficient savings to improve their economic situation at home. Recruited by labor agents to man America's mills, mines, factories, and foundries, most remained for good, earning a living for themselves and their families, creating opportunity for their children, and providing the muscle and skill that fueled North America's industrial revolution.

Despite the industrial sector's need for labor, the immigrants who provided it faced a great deal of prejudice. Nativism, the extolling of "true" American values based on the culture of the original British colonies, surged with the increase in immigration. Prejudice was nothing new in America; earlier arrivals, such as the Irish, had to contend with discrimination and signs in shop and factory windows that proclaimed: No Irish Need Apply. But the Irish had at least had the advantage of speaking English, and many members of other groups, such as the Scandinavians and the Germans, shared their Protestant faith with the American majority. Even after several decades in America, some of these groups, especially the Irish, had only been able to climb to just above the bottom rung of the economic ladder, and their hold there was precarious. Not surprisingly, they regarded the new immigrants as a threat to their tenuous position.

*Because the years between 1880 and 1914 were a period of rapid industrialization in the United States and Canada, many of the Serbian immigrants of that time found work in factories and mines. Shown here is a group of Minnesota mine workers, Serbs among them, in 1910.*

Because most took jobs as industrial laborers, the new immigrants were often blamed for the social disruptions caused by industrialization. Americans comfortable with the image of the United States as a peaceful agrarian democracy were troubled by the new industrial world of fire and smoke, thundering machinery, labor unions, strikes, and scabs. The growth in unionization and the increase in strikes were blamed on "anarchists" and "socialists" among the "foreigners." Professors, journalists, ministers, and politicians decried the pollution of the American bloodline and culture. Despite the promises engraved on the Statue of Liberty, America was not sure that it wanted these huddled masses at all.

Most of the approximately 100,000 Serbs who arrived in the United States between 1880 and 1914 were classic great-wave immigrants—uneducated single males in their teens or early twenties who came to America with less than $25 in their pockets. Serbian peasants are fond of the aphorism *Covek mora da radi* (A person has to work), and the great-wave Serbs certainly embodied this ethic. Like other great-wave immigrants, they were willing to toil long hours at dangerous and low-paying industrial jobs in order to save enough money with which to start anew in the homeland. Because they planned to stay in North America only temporarily, they referred to their settlements here as "colonies."

The largest old-settler colonies developed in the industrial heartland, where work was to be had in factories, mines, and mills: in Toronto and Windsor, Ontario; in and around Pittsburgh, Pennsylvania; in Lackawanna, New York; and in Chicago, Illinois, and Milwaukee, Wisconsin. A significant number of Serbian immigrants found homes in isolated mining communities, such as Chisolm, Minnesota, and Ely, Nevada. Many were itinerant, traveling from one colony to another to pursue work. By 1910, old settlers had developed a network of neighborhoods from Elizabeth, New Jersey, to San Francisco, California.

Serbs from a particular region in Europe tended to settle with others from the same region. For example, Pennsylvania was home to large numbers of Serbs from the Croatian territories of Lika and Kordun. Others from Lika and Montenegro settled in Chicago. Serbs from the Vojvodina region settled with others from that area. In this way, the distribution and character of the North American Serbs mirrored that of the Serbian population in the Old World. Later generations have tended to maintain the same settlement patterns. As a result, although the Serbian-American population is relatively small in sheer numbers, it remains remarkably cohesive and concentrated.

Like their predecessors, the young immigrants of the great wave almost all originated outside of Serbia proper. Estimates vary, but at least two-thirds came from settlements in the Hapsburg territories neighboring Serbia, such as the Dalmatian coast, the Croatian provinces of Lika and Slavonia, and the Vojvodina region northeast of Belgrade. In most cases, they had settled in these regions generations earlier, after fleeing Turkish rule in Serbia proper. Many were the descendants of the Granicari, who, since the 16th century, had formed a military and population buffer between the Hapsburg and Ottoman empires. For 300

*A Serbian immigrant and her two children look over their garden, located near the Pioneer Mine in Minnesota, in 1922. Such gardens were usually practical rather than ornamental; they were used to grow food for the family's table.*

years, they had enjoyed general political and religious freedom in return for military service against the Turks and other enemies of the Hapsburgs, but by the late 19th century, most of the Austro-Hungarian territories where the Serbs had settled had been devastated by a depression that left the richer Hapsburg territories of the north unable to support the predominantly agricultural Slavic regions. Markets dried up, and money grew scarce. Inheritance laws that required land to be distributed among all the sons of a family, instead of to just the oldest, led to smaller and smaller plots that were eventually inadequate to support their owners. Serbian peasants were not represented in the Hapsburg government, and they were taxed exorbitantly. In Slavonia and Vojvodina, many were forced to work as laborers on huge estates for impossibly low wages. Periodic crop failures added to the misery and helped make the factories of Pittsburgh and elsewhere look very attractive.

Ethnic and religious persecution also drove Serbs to America. By the late 19th century the Hapsburgs had terminated their centuries-old agreement with the Granicari, who were then absorbed into the larger populations of the territories where they lived. In Vojvodina, they were subjected to the Magyarization campaign of their Hungarian overlords. (Hungarians are known as Magyars.) The government tried to substitute Hungarian for Serbian as the official language of schools and courts and sought to force Serbian conversion to Roman Catholicism. Once Serbia gained its independence from the Ottoman Empire, Serbs within the Hapsburg Empire were seen as a source of potential subversion. In Croatia, the pressure to convert to Roman Catholicism came not only from the Hungarian government but also from the Croatians, some of whom called their Serbian neighbors "Orthodox Croatians."

Very few Serbs from Serbia proper left for North America at this time. The peasants there still worked large family farms connected through a collective village system known as *zadruga*, and they fared significantly better than their compatriots elsewhere. Serbia's emergence as an independent nation provided them with more incentive to stay, and because so few of the pioneers had been from the homeland itself, few peasants there had heard the enticing tales of life in America that seemed to lure the population of entire regions of Dalmatia to the New World.

## The Journey

No matter what their motivation, most old-settler Serbians made their way to the New World in the crowded steerage compartments of steamships. After leaving the port city of Trieste or Fiume, a typical immigrant spent about two weeks in the huge, poorly ventilated cargo compartments that the lowest-priced ticket purchased. Access to the deck was limited, and the close quarters bred disease. After 1891, immigrants were subject to medical examinations on both sides of the crossing. A small percentage were refused passage or entry; those who passed inspection watched as steamship officials doused their baggage with disinfectant.

Some of the penniless arrivals knew where to go after being processed at the U.S. immigration center at Ellis Island, in New York harbor. They had relatives to seek out or the addresses of friends from their village who had arrived earlier. Others knew only that they wanted work and were recruited at dockside by labor brokers to work on farms and in industry. Brokers often took advantage of these "greenhorns." Although many newly arrived Serbs found helping hands in America, there was no shortage of confidence men and other predators ready to snare the unwary newcomer.

One of the most articulate of the greenhorns was Michael Pupin, a physicist and inventor whose Pulitzer Prize–winning autobiography, *From Immigrant to Inventor*, was published in 1926. Although he arrived in 1874, before most old settlers, Pupin's story is typical of the great-wave Serb.

He was born in 1855 in the region of Banat, which was then controlled by Hungary. His father, a Granicari, never forgave the Hapsburgs for dissolving the frontier zone in 1869. He passed on his nationalistic

This Serbian family was photographed at Ellis Island in the late
19th century soon after its
arrival in the United States.
Easily distinguished by their
dress and lack of knowledge of
the English language and
American customs, newly arrived
immigrants were easy targets for
swindlers and bigots.

fervor to his son, who fought for Slavic independence
even as he was rising through the Austro-Hungarian
university system. While in Prague on scholarship, he
demonstrated for Czech independence, seeing in this
cause an echo of Serbia's struggle. When he wrangled
with German classmates, he was threatened with ex-
pulsion, despite his promising intellect.

When his father died, the young Pupin looked for
a way to make money for his family. As he describes
it, he sailed for America "with just one suit of clothes
on my back, a few changes of linen, and a red Turkish

fez which nobody would buy." Although better educated than most, Pupin also looked upon the New World as a short-range prospect; in his autobiography he explains: "I promised I would return rich in rare knowledge and honors." Like many others, he did not actually return for decades.

His passage was typically dismal. He found a tiny space on the deck of his ship because he could not afford a mattress and blanket for his steerage bunk. His memoirs detail the trials of the journey:

> If it had not been for the warm smokestack, I would have died of cold. At first I had to fight for my place there in the daytime, but when the immigrants understood that I had no warm clothing they did not disturb me any longer. . . . A blast of the everlasting gales had carried away my hat, and a Turkish fez such as the Serbs of Bosnia wear was the only headgear I had. It was providential that I had not succeeded in selling it in Prague. Most of my fellow immigrants thought I was a Turk and cared little about my discomforts. But, nevertheless, I felt quite brave and strong in the daytime; at night, however, when, standing alone alongside of the smokestack, I beheld through the howling darkness the white rims of the mountain-high waves speeding on like maddened dragons toward the tumbling ship, my heart sank low.

The 15 year old landed at Castle Rock, New York, with dreams about Benjamin Franklin and his kite and the equivalent of five cents in his pocket. In the New World, he was able to turn those dreams into a lifetime of study and renown as a physicist. The five cents, though, was the instrument of a bitter lesson:

> A piece of prune pie caught my eye, and no true Serb can resist the allurements of prunes. It is a national sweetmeat. I bought it, paying five cents for it, the only money I had, and then I made a bee-line across Battery Park, at the same time

attending to my pie. My first bargain proved to be a failure. The prune pie was a deception; it was a prune pie filled with prune pits, and I thought of the words of my fellow passenger on the immigrant ship who had said, "No matter who you are or what you know or what you have, you will be a greenhorn when you land in America."

Besides being easy prey for swindlers, Serbian greenhorns were victims of the same prejudice that greeted other great-wave immigrants. They were often lumped together with other eastern Europeans and labeled "bohunks" or "hunkies." (The first term derives from Bohemian; the second from Hungarian.) Because most worked as unskilled laborers, they were widely held to be unfit for all but brute physical work and were stereotyped as strong backed, hard drinking, irascible, and slow witted. Most worked long hours under dangerous and even brutalizing conditions; out-

*A turn-of-the-century mining operation near Butte, Montana, 1,900 feet below the surface.*

side of the workplace, Serbs most often kept to themselves, partly by choice, partly because they were excluded from other groups.

The experience of Milan Mileusnich, a great-wave Serb whose story was told by Milka Licina in the leading Serbian periodical, *Serb World*, is not atypical. In 1910, Mileusnich left his home in the Croatian province of Lika, where he had been a peasant farmer. After crossing the Atlantic, he worked for two years in the Pennsylvania coal mines under grueling conditions:

> He moved through the dark, dank underground mine corridors digging coal, sometimes in water up to his hips, knowing that sudden death lurked in coal damp blasts and cave-ins. He worked in a mine when there was work, and there was never a nickel in his pocket after he paid the fixed price for gum boots, work clothes, and the bare essentials of living. He worked from daybreak to sundown, and when the long day ended, grimed from head to toe, he came home to the miserable clapboard shanties where he boarded with his fellow Serbs.

Most old-settler Serbs began their lives in America in similar circumstances: laboring under dangerous, if not deadly, conditions, earning a subsistence wage that paid for ramshackle housing. Single men often lived in boardinghouses run by the wives of married workers, often renting a bed for a single eight-hour shift. Three men would share the bed over 24 hours; 2 worked while the other slept.

One day, Mileusnich received a letter from a friend that seemed to promise deliverance. "Brother Milan, in Iowa the corn grows as tall as in the Old Country, and the farm girls' cheeks are as rosy as our own maidens' back home," it read. The alluring imagery was enough; the next day Mileusnich quit the mine and hopped a freight train to farm country, where he spent a satisfying year tilling the Iowa soil. He worked for a German family who valued his labor, and his relations with them were "harmonious, but not familiar." Even-

*In order to save money, Serbian immigrants often lived in boardinghouses owned and operated by their countrymen, such as this one photographed near Eveleth, Minnesota, in 1905.*

tually, the farmer developed a deep respect for Milan, whom he called Mike, because the young Serb worked hard, had good values, and spoke vividly of his Serbian background. One day, in an expansive frame of mind, the farmer hinted at the possibility that Mike might marry Clara, his oldest daughter. The surprised Mileusnich was overwhelmed by the freedom of America, where, unlike Europe, a peasant could dream of owning a farm and even of marrying the landowner's daughter. But as was true for many immigrants, the promise exceeded the reality. The next day, Mileusnich overheard the farmer and his wife arguing:

"But Helga," the farmer said, "most of the farm boys are leaving the farm and are going to the big cities. And Mike is a good worker, one who loves the land."

"No!" cried the farm woman. "Clara is not for an alien and . . . a greenhorn!"

The farmer responded firmly. "Mike is dependable and trustworthy, an intelligent man who will quickly learn our American customs and language."

"No! Our daughter shall not marry a foreigner . . . a hunky!"

The irony, of course, is that the farmer and his wife were probably either immigrants or the children of immigrants themselves. Mileusnich lasted out the harvest and then headed east to find industrial employment among other Serbs.

But for all the hardship Serbian immigrants faced, most endured and found a degree of freedom and opportunity in North America unavailable to them in their homeland. As their numbers grew, Serbs established communities, and settlers could count on finding whole blocks in such cities as Pittsburgh and Chicago where only Serbian was spoken, where they could buy from Serb merchants, read Serbian newspapers, and—after the turn of the century—worship in Serbian churches. These communities were a piece of the old country in the New World, and they helped ease the adjustment of the next major wave of immigrants.

*Faced with political and economic turmoil at home in the years immediately following World War II, many Serbs sought to emigrate. In 1959 the émigrés in this photograph were stranded for five months aboard a Danish freighter before receiving their travel papers.*

# AFTER THE GREAT WAVE

The great wave of immigration, Serbian and otherwise, ended with World War I, when the turmoil in Europe and on the Atlantic made travel unsafe. Those Serbs who did relocate during wartime were more likely to be repatriates returning home to fight for their country than immigrants. Two hundred sixty-four Serbian Americans from Milwaukee returned to fight in the Serbian army on the Salonika front; only one is known to have returned to America.

During the interwar years, many factors combined to prevent a renewed mass migration of Serbs. The creation of the Kingdom of the Serbs, Croats, and Slovenes gave reason for optimism about Serbia's future, as did the leading role taken by Serbia in the new alliance. The war had magnified American suspicion of foreigners, and nativists scored major political victories with the implementation of restrictive immigration laws in 1921 and 1924. The new legislation established a "national origins" system that set strict annual quotas for each nationality based on a percentage of the

*During World War I, hundreds of Serbian Americans—including those pictured here—returned to the old country to fight in the Serbian army.*

total of that nationality already living in the United States. The 1921 law set a quota of two percent of the 1910 census, and the 1924 law was even more restrictive: By making the 1890 census the basis for a three percent quota, the 1924 act clearly favored the northern and western European groups who had arrived earlier in the 19th century. As a result, the annual quota for all Yugoslav immigrants was set at only 671 per year. Although the quota was later raised to 942, the law remained an effective barrier. By contrast, Canada's immigration laws remained relatively permissive, and the number of Serbian immigrants to Canada swelled during the interwar years.

The Serbian-American community was also hard hit by the depression that battered the American and world economy during the 1920s and the 1930s. The decline in American industrial production greatly affected old-settler communities, and a number of Serbs were forced to return in discouragement to the old country. Because of Prohibition, even the numerous tavern owners among the Serbs saw their businesses suffer dramatically.

## The Newcomers

It was not until the decade after World War II that a new wave of Serbian settlers arrived on American shores. This postwar wave of Serbian immigrants, the *novidosli*, or newcomers, was driven to emigrate because of changes resulting from World War II. Most were refugees from a continent ravaged by military and political struggle and either could not, or would not, return to Yugoslavia. They included large numbers of former Yugoslav army officers, officers and troops who had been German prisoners of war, workers who had been deported to Germany by the Nazi invaders, former Yugoslav government officials, and former Četniks, who, as the losers of a civil war with Tito's Partisans, were not welcome in the new Yugoslavia. The newcomers' admittance was made possible by new legislation in both the United States and Canada that allowed those countries to provide asylum to persons displaced by the war.

The most numerous and perhaps the most cohesive group within the broader category delineated as newcomers was the Četniks. Many arrived still angry at having lost control of postwar Yugoslavia to the Communists and at what they regarded as their betrayal by the Allies, who had originally recognized the Četnik leader Draža Mihajlović as the official leader of the Yugoslav government in exile but had shifted their support to the Partisans when it became clear that Tito's forces constituted a more formidable fighting unit. In the United States and Canada, the Četniks continued to fight Yugoslav Communism, largely through the dissemination of information and by forming political organizations designed to promote awareness of Yugoslav issues. In a number of cities today, these former

*Between the two world wars, Canada's immigration laws were more permissive than those of the United States, prompting many Europeans to move there. This group of Yugoslav emigrants was photographed en route to Ottawa in 1938.*

soldiers, though elderly, continue to maintain that work toward attaining their long-standing goal of a non-Communist Yugoslavia.

Virtually all of the newcomers shared an enmity toward the Federative People's Republic of Yugoslavia. Other military opponents to the new regime among the newcomers ranged from members of the defeated Yugoslav army to members of the ultra-right-wing nationalist corps that had maintained order in Serbia for the Nazi occupiers. These *Ljoticevci*, organized by Dmitrije Ljotic, settled for the most part in Milwaukee. Even those newcomers without a military background—former members of the royal government, dispossessed landowners and members of the middle and upper classes under the monarchy, and a variety of professionals—vehemently opposed Tito, and their presence helped infuse Serbian-American communities with an intense political awareness. Like the old settlers, most of the newcomers considered themselves sojourners, but it was political change rather than the attainment of economic security that they were awaiting before returning home. Those changes, of course, have not occurred, and their children and grandchildren have assumed permanent roles in North American society.

Most newcomers settled in or near existing Serbian-American communities, which often sponsored their immigration and provided financial and spiritual support. The newcomers, in turn, revitalized these communities. They joined churches and clubs and founded their own organizations. A glance at a recent issue of the *Srbobran*, the official paper of the Serbian National Federation (SNF), with its notices of Četnik picnics in several cities and an article commemorating the 90th anniversary of Mihajlović's birth, gives some indication of the newcomers' influence.

The newcomers believed strongly in national purity, or "Serbianism" (srpstvo). They resisted many of the trends toward Americanization that they found in the Serbian-American communities, such as the use of English in Orthodox services, the use of pews (Orthodox worshipers traditionally stand in church), and the neglect of the Serbian language within the community. They also encouraged a new emphasis on authenticity, such as the use of traditional costumes, on the part of Serbian folklore, dance, and choral groups.

Although the newcomers contributed greatly to the preservation of Serbian culture in America, they did not merge easily with earlier immigrant groups and their descendants. Most were more politically aware, better educated, more established professionally, and financially better off than the old settlers. Unable to accept the comparatively poor economic position of Serbs within American society, they rebelled against the control exercised by the old-settler leadership. Many placed a greater emphasis on assimilation than had their predecessors and preferred to see their fellow Serbs only at professional conventions or at small dinner parties among friends.

The arrival of the newcomers raised questions of identity that many longer-established Serbian Americans believed had been long resolved. Working-class newcomers often stood apart in dress and manner from the old settlers and their descendants. They dressed "foreign," spoke Serbian instead of English, and preferred accordion music to the *tamburitza* music popular among the great-wave immigrants. As survivors of one of history's worst wars, they brought both new energy and a confusing diversity to the Serbian communities of North America.

## The Recent Arrivals

Despite the exceptions allowed for displaced persons, the exclusionary quota system remained the immigration law of the United States until 1965, when the Hart-Celler Act eliminated nationality as a criterion for legal entry. This change opened the door to the latest wave of Serbian immigrants, the recent arrivals.

Each generation of Serbian immigrants has planned to return to the homeland, yet for many Serbian Americans this dream has remained just that. By contrast, the recent arrivals actually do constitute something of a Serbian colony in the New World. Following the time-honored Yugoslav practice of *pechalba*, or foreign work stay, many recent arrivals return home after 1,

*In 1965 the Hart-Celler Act eliminated nationality as a criterion for legal entry into the United States, opening the door to a new wave of Serbian immigrants. Seen here in October 1967 are Gruja Apostovic (far left) and his wife, Desanka (far right), with their children, as they receive the documentation that will allow them to become permanent residents of the United States.*

10, or even 20 years with money to spend and skills to market. Since their tie to the New World is primarily economic, they do not form a cohesive group. Many maintain dual citizenship. Some work for Yugoslav enterprises, some for North American. Whereas some are professionals, others are working class. They may vacation in Yugoslavia or send their children to visit with relatives back home. They follow the latest Serbian news, popular music, and soccer scores. This phenomenon is not confined to the United States or Canada; Serbian sojourners can be found around the globe.

The experience of the recent arrivals does have some elements in common with that of their compatriots who preceded them to North America. One such recent arrival has described his life as a Serbian with connections to both the Old and the New World. His father was a successful businessman who had worked for both American and Yugoslav mining companies, yet as a teenager Michael (not his real name) learned that he was not a "normal" American. Because his family name sounds Slavic, his elementary school classmates teased him about being a Communist, and he learned to avoid wearing any red-colored clothing, even a tie or handkerchief, for fear that he would be taunted for being a "red." Although he was an excellent student and in time would build a career as an electrical engineer, he remembers how, at a school contest held on an American military base, the organizer joked about having "those kinds of names" on the program. Whereas such remarks seem a lesser obstacle to overcome than the nativist barriers erected against the immigrants of the great wave and while this young man has had educational and economic opportunities that children of the old settlers would have envied, the frequent reminders that he was not a "typical" American still hurt.

He and his family remained proud of their Serbian heritage. As children, he and his sister attended a weekend Serbian school in Queens, New York, operated by the Yugoslav consulate for members of the colony. There they learned about Serbian history and culture and studied Serbo-Croatian. Rather than forming contacts within the nearby working-class communities in their home state of New Jersey, they tended to get together with other colony children to socialize and talk about the latest Serbian singers or styles. As adults, they perform in a Yugoslav dance ensemble in New York and return frequently to Serbia. Although proud of their Serbian identity, they refer to themselves as "Yugoslav" in origin; unlike the postwar wave, they accept the concept of the Yugoslav state.

For more than 150 years now Serbian Americans have struggled to define their identity in terms of both the new society in which they live and the old order that has been left behind. For the children and grandchildren of immigrants, the question of identity has often been even harder to settle. Although the younger generations may have had little firsthand knowledge of the old country, they are often caught between parents and grandparents determined to see that old values are retained by their offspring and the American ways they learn in school and on television. Despite the changes it has undergone, the Serbian-American community has been successful in maintaining a number of institutions, the Orthodox church the most important among them, that have helped it hold on to those traditions and values that are most Serbian.

# ONLY UNITY WILL SAVE THE SERBS

M any Serbs proudly display the symbol of the four S's on their embroidery, jewelry, books, and banners. These S's (which in the Cyrillic alphabet look like the English letter C) stand for the phrase *Samo Sloga Srbina Spassava* (Only Unity Will Save the Serbs), a slogan symbolizing Serbian resistance to absorption by foreign cultures. Although their rich national and folk heritage has helped them remain distinct, survival as a people, in both the Old World and the New, would have been impossible without the organizations that bind Serbian communities together.

The most vital Serbian-American organizations, the SNF and the Serbian Orthodox church in America, were begun by immigrants who had arrived during the second great wave. Young and unskilled, without the comfort of family and friends, surrounded by foreign languages, religions, and customs, and scattered across a broad continent, Serbs turned to each other for financial assistance, advice, and companionship. It took years, though, for Serbian communities to grow large enough to create supportive institutions for their members.

*A prominent businessman and Serbian-American activist, Joe Melich, on horseback, drills 250 uniformed members of the local Serbian lodge in Bingham Canyon, Utah, in the early 20th century.*

## Every Bird Flies to Its Own Nest

Serbian Americans formed their first fraternal organizations even before they built their first churches. Initially, Serbs joined fraternals that served other Slavic groups as well, such as the Slavonic Illyrian Benevolent Organization, founded in San Francisco in 1857. This association served South Slavs, primarily Croats and Serbs, and made a point of reaching out to those who had settled in remote mining and agricultural communities. It aided visiting sailors in need, paid funeral expenses for its members, and even arranged return trips to the old country for those who were terminally ill.

In the days before labor unions and protective social legislation, immigrant groups also formed fraternal organizations to protect the workingman. Conditions in the mines and foundries were little short of murderous, and dismemberment and death were not uncommon, yet few employers were willing to provide any kind of disability or health insurance. By paying small monthly dues to a fraternal lodge, a member could buy modest life and accident insurance. At first, Serbs joined already existing fraternals that provided these services, but in time they formed their own organizations, using the older groups established by the Germans, Irish, Italians, Slovaks, and Croatians as models. The first Serbian lodge in the East was formed in 1897 in McKeesport, Pennsylvania. By 1900, nine more Serbian lodges were nominally in existence, but these were sponsored by the Russian Federation. Even though the Serbs were linked to the Russians by their common faith, they were in need of an independent federation—as Serbs say, "Every bird flies to its own nest."

The Serbian nest came into being in 1901 in Wilkes-Barre, Pennsylvania, at which point the nine Serbian lodges broke off to form the first purely Serbian federation. Despite opposition from rival fraternals, Serbian lodges proliferated. In 1929, the three largest of these united as the SNF, and since then this Pittsburgh-based organization has been at the center of the fraternal movement. Further centralization occurred with the merger in 1963 of the large Cleveland organization Jedinstvo (Unity) and the SNF.

The lodges provided, and continue to provide, economic benefits, but they have been equally significant as social and political organizations. Although the SNF in 1929 was able to offer its members a death benefit of only $1,000, it aimed to supply Serbs with something much more important than money: a sense of community and identity. In the words of Sava Hajdin, the founder of the fraternal that developed into the SNF, "[We] never wanted our organization to be just a federation of fraternal lodges. We wanted to be the *matica* [guardian] of Serbs in America, and a confirmation of Serbian Orthodox ideals."

Hajdin would no doubt be proud of the role played by his federation in this century. For 80 years, the SNF and related organizations have directed the energies of the Serbian community. During World War I, it cooperated with the Serbian National Defense (SND), an organization founded by Michael Pupin and others, to provide aid to the homeland. The SNF recruited soldiers for the Serbian army and sent funds in support of the Serbian Red Cross. During World War II, the SNF collected and shipped donations to help the Allies, and both during and after the war, federation leaders sent relief to Serbian refugees and prisoners of

*This meeting of the Serbian-Montenegrin Benevolent Society was photographed in San Francisco in 1915. During World War I, the Serbian population in the Bay Area dwindled as hundreds returned home to fight in the Serbian army.*

war. After the war, the SNF sponsored thousands of displaced persons who wanted to come to North America and helped them once they had arrived.

The SNF has proved itself a faithful guardian of Serbian culture both in its homeland and in the New World. In North America, besides providing insurance, the SNF has contributed to innumerable building and scholarship funds within Serbian communities from coast to coast. These include the mortgage funds for a Serbian Orthodox Seminary in Libertyville, Illinois, the Nikola Tesla and Michael Pupin scholarship funds, and a fund for the printing and free distribution of Serbian primers so that young people in the United States and Canada might learn their ancestral language. At present, the SNF is raising funds through its weekly newspaper for the restoration of the St. Vraćar Cathedral.

From the beginning, the fraternal lodges served as a social focus of the Serbian-American communities, places where Serbs could meet after work and on weekends for a drink and conversation in their own language. The federation continues to play this role today, on a national as well as a local level. It sponsors tournaments for golf, bowling, soccer, tennis, and other sports and a three-day Serbian Days celebration every summer. Many Serbs—even those who have been in this country for 50 years—treasure these events as a time to renew aspects of themselves and their community that would otherwise be lost.

A typical setting for these ritual affirmations of Serbian community might be a bowling alley outside Harrisburg, Pennsylvania, with two live orchestras and an abundance of food and drink on hand; the bowling is secondary to remembering friends and heritage. As one participant put it, "The athletic reason is irrelevant—the congregating is all important." Such tournaments and athletic contests help the federation impart a sense of community identity to each new generation in America.

The federation's weekly, the *Srbobran*, which dates from 1906, publicizes and promotes a variety of such community events—from SNF-sponsored contests and

*(continued on page 73)*

# SRPSTVO — BEING SERBIAN

Overleaf: *During the Easter season, worshipers at a Serbian Orthodox church in New York City examine an icon and colorfully decorated eggs. The Serbian Orthodox church is perhaps the most important institution that unifies the Serbian-American community, and Easter and other holy days are occasions for Serbians to join together in celebration and remembrance.*

Icons, or traditional religious images like the ones behind the altar in the photo at left, are one of the distinguishing features of Serbian and other Orthodox churches. Candles are lit (above) in remembrance of the dead, in veneration of a saint, or to symbolize penance or special prayers. For many, the Serbian Orthodox church is the very essence of srpstvo, or being Serbian, and it continues to unite old and new generations (right).

*Serbian Orthodox churches serve the community as social centers as well as houses of worship. At a gathering in the basement of a Serbian Orthodox church on Chicago's North Side, young communicants (left, below) enjoy delicious baked rolls and bread (left, below and above), then listen to an accordion trio performing traditional Serbian music (above).*

*Attired in traditional costumes, a Serbian-American youth group performs folk dances of the homeland following a church dinner in Chicago. The many cultural and religious organizations formed by Serbian Americans have enabled them to preserve their rich cultural heritage.*

*Two Serbian-American youths at play on the grounds of the Monastery of St. Sava in Libertyville, Illinois. For the younger generation, being Serbian is as much a pleasure as it is a solemn duty.*

*Serbian Americans shoot pool at the Serbian club in Aliquippa, Pennsylvania, in January 1941. Lodges and clubhouses often served as the social centers of the Serbian-American community.*

*(continued from page 64)*

festivals and church anniversaries to the profusion of picnics that fill the Serbian summer. A column entitled "Reflections" keeps readers abreast of Serbs in the news, and articles appear regularly on developments in the church, both here and in Yugoslavia. The paper publishes wedding announcements and obituaries as well as advertisements for everything from Bibles to lamb rotisseries.

## The Religious Tie

The SNF has done much to maintain and unite the Serbian communities of North America. Yet these efforts have been successful only because they have been built around the central pillar of Serbian identity, the Serbian Orthodox church. Serbian Orthodoxy defines Serbian identity in the New World and the Old; without their church, Serbs, whether active believers or not, would lose touch with their fundamental sense of who they are.

To appreciate fully the centrality of the church in Serbian culture today, one must look briefly at its pivotal role in Serbia's history. Serbians belong to the

*This photograph of Saints Constantine and Helen Serbian and Greek Orthodox Church and Rectory was taken in Galveston, Texas, in 1935. Galveston was the site of one of the earliest Serbian Orthodox churches to be established in America.*

Eastern Orthodox branch of Christianity and write in the Cyrillic rather than in the Latin alphabet. This is because their ancestors were converted by missionaries of the Eastern or Byzantine church, then based in Constantinople.

These missionaries were followers of two saints, known as the "Apostles to the Slavs," Methodius and Cyril. The alphabet, named for Cyril and developed by him and his followers, allowed Eastern Orthodox missions to translate religious texts directly into Slavonic, the language of South Slavs at that time. This ability to use the native language of the people, the vernacular, gave Byzantine missionaries an edge over missionaries from Rome, whose work among the South Slav tribes was less successful because of their use of Latin. As a result, in the 9th century, the Byzantine missionaries conducted mass christenings in which the loosely organized Serbian tribes were converted to Orthodoxy.

The Serbian Orthodox church was founded as a distinct branch of Eastern Orthodoxy by Saint Sava in 1217. Its language, rituals, and teachings have kept the Serbian identity alive, whether in the golden age of Serbia, when monasteries and religious art flourished, in a Serbia conquered and occupied by Islamic invaders (the Ottoman Turks), among the exile communities who fled the Turks to settle in Croatia or Hungary, within the Yugoslav kingdom of the interwar period, and even within the officially atheist Yugoslavia of today. The Orthodox church continues as well to be the touchstone of identity for Serbians in North America.

Both customs and doctrine distinguish Orthodoxy from the Protestant and Catholic faiths that predominate in America. One fundamental difference is the calendar. The Serbian Orthodox church continues to use the Julian calendar, which is 13 days behind the Gregorian calendar devised by Pope Gregory in 1582 and used in most of the Western world. (For instance, Orthodox Christmas falls on January 7 rather than on December 25.)

Orthodox worshipers venerate traditional religious paintings called icons and believe these images have the transcendental power to link humans with God. Some Orthodox worshipers believe that icons can work miracles. A visitor to an Orthodox church might be startled to see worshipers burning candles in front of them or even kneeling down before the icons and kissing them. These people are worshiping God through the images, not the images themselves. This visitor might also be surprised to meet the priest's wife—unlike Catholic priests, Orthodox priests are allowed to marry.

Orthodoxy means "correct worship," and Serbs do resist changes in church doctrine, believing in the preservation of their rituals and traditions, which were for-

*The interior of St. George's Serbian Orthodox Church in Duluth, Minnesota, in 1939. On its walls hang the religious pictures, or icons, that are central to Orthodox worship.*

mulated by the first fathers of the church back in the earliest Christian communities. They deny the Roman Catholic doctrine of the infallibility of the pope and dispute his claim to rule over all Christian churches. Instead, they believe that the church should be headed by a council of bishops. Orthodoxy strongly emphasizes community among believers, and that value has remained particularly strong among Serbian-American immigrants and their descendants.

The first pioneer Serbs were so few in number that, rather than congregating independently, they looked for a church among the larger Greek and Russian communities. The earliest congregation known to include large numbers of Serbs was the Greek Holy Trinity Church, established in New Orleans in 1864. Serbs were members of Orthodox churches in San Francisco and Galveston as well. The first independent Serbian church was founded in Jackson, California, in 1893, but Orthodoxy would take root most firmly in the East. By 1900, the first Serbian church east of the Mississippi had been founded in McKeesport, Pennsylvania. Steelton, Pennsylvania, followed suit three years later. Church growth corresponded to the increasing numbers of Serbian immigrants, and within a short time Serbian Orthodox churches could be found in most Serbian communities from Chicago to New York. Although these congregations were predominantly Serbian and were led by Serbian priests, many of them drew Orthodox worshipers of Greek, Russian, Romanian, or Macedonian backgrounds.

Steelton parishioners recall a baptism performed at the church there for a clan of Orthodox Gypsies, who presented homemade copper artifacts in exchange for the service and then invited the congregation to a christening party at the Gypsy camp. The fervor of early Orthodox immigrants made up for their sparse numbers; history had taught them to cling tightly to their faith.

Serbs struggled to remain not only distinctly Orthodox but also independent of larger, non-Serbian Orthodox groups. Because Alaska had been a Russian colony until 1868, there was a sizable Russian population on the Pacific Coast in the 19th century and an established Russian Orthodox church in the New World dating back to the 1700s. It made sense for the earliest Serbian immigrants to worship with their fellow Orthodox Slavs, and many attended Russian churches until distinctly Serbian congregations were established. Even the predominantly Serbian churches remained under the authority of the Russian Orthodox church in Moscow until 1921, when the Serbian patriarch created the Diocese of the United States and Canada.

The life of one early church figure illustrates well both the connection between the Serbian and Russian churches and the Serbs' ongoing struggle for independence. The Reverend Sebastian Dabovich (1863–1940) spent his long life as an apostle to Serbs across America. He founded churches, visited remote families to bring them the sacraments of their faith, and traveled around the world in the cause of Orthodoxy. By some reports, he crossed the Atlantic Ocean 15 times and the Pacific 9 times.

Dabovich was the first Serbian Orthodox priest born in America. His father, Ilija Dabovich, had been a pioneer in the San Francisco community, having arrived from Sasovici, Herzegovina. The son received his religious training through the Russian Orthodox church, first in California and then in Russia itself. He rose within the ranks of the Russian Orthodox church until he was appointed in 1905 to head the Serbian Orthodox church mission in the United States.

Despite his deep-seated ties to Russia, Dabovich struggled to maintain a respectful distance from the parent church. He resisted Russian efforts to establish a Russian charter for the first Serbian church in Jackson, California, and asserted his independence in working among European and native populations in Alaska, where a Serbian church, St. Sava, was built despite Russian opposition.

In 1907, the Russian archbishop for America wanted to appoint Dabovich to the position of Russian bishop for the Serbian people. Although the Serbians held Dabovich in high regard, most opposed his ap-

*Father Sebastian Dabovich was the first American-born Serbian Orthodox priest. Although educated in the Russian Orthodox tradition, his life's work was directed toward the promulgation of an independent Serbian Orthodox church in America.*

pointment to this office because of their firm commitment to the founding of an independent Serbian church. Dabovich worked instead to establish an independent Serbian parish in Chicago, where he served as its first parish priest. The Serbian Orthodox Church of the Resurrection would later be founded in this same location. While in Chicago, Dabovich also started the first Serbian-American church newspaper, the *Herald of the Orthodox Church Mission*.

In 1918, Dabovich left Chicago to resume his missionary work and traveled as far as Japan, often penniless himself, to administer to the Serbian Orthodox community. He died in Yugoslavia in 1940, having given 53 years of his life to the church.

In the meantime, other Serbian Americans had been striving to establish their own church. In Pittsburgh in 1906, Serbian priests met as a group for the first time. After a decade of internal struggle, the priests had succeeded in organizing their parishes into districts, thereby paving the way for the election of a separate Serbian bishop. In 1917, Reverend Mardary Uskokovich, a Montenegrin monk trained by the Russians, arrived in North America. Uskokovich rose quickly to become the head of the Serbian diocese within the Russian church. He was designated bishop-elect in 1919 and soon persuaded the Patriarch of the Serbian church to create a separate Serbian Orthodox Diocese of North America and Canada. Five years later, he himself became the bishop of the new diocese.

Uskokovich devoted a plot of land in Libertyville, Illinois, to the needs of his new church. He built a facility there that functioned at first as an orphanage and later became the seat of the newly formed Serbian Orthodox Diocese. In addition, the Monastery of St. Sava was erected there in 1931, followed by a children's camp and a seminary 11 years later. This and two other church holdings, in Shadeland, Pennsylvania, and Jackson, California, remain important locations for church and social gatherings to this day.

In the years since its founding, the Serbian Diocese has helped Serbs in America maintain connections with their countrymen elsewhere. When Serbia was devastated by invasion and oppression during World War II, the church called attention to the suffering in the homeland and worked together with the SND to organize a relief effort. After the war, the church sponsored refugees to the United States and helped organize relief for those remaining in Europe. Today, the church continues to remind Serbs of who they are by fighting for the rights of the churches and churchgoers within Communist Yugoslavia.

Over the past 25 years, the Serbian community has proved the strength of its attachment to its religion in another, more painful way. In 1963, the Serbian Diocese of North America and Canada split into two factions, one favoring allegiance to the patriarchy in Belgrade, the other advocating independence for the Serbian Orthodox church in North America. This controversy divided communities, congregations, and even families across the continent. The scars left by the split have only recently begun to heal as passions cool and people begin to take hesitant steps toward a reconciliation.

The trouble began in 1962 when the Holy Synod, the council that, along with the patriarch, rules the Orthodox church in Belgrade, began investigating reports concerning Bishop Dionisije. Dionisije, who had headed the North American Diocese since 1940, had allegedly misused church property and conducted his personal life in a manner unbefitting an Orthodox priest. When Dionisije refused to attend a hearing on these very serious charges, the Synod suspended him and reorganized his sprawling jurisdiction into three regional dioceses, appointing an independent bishop to head each one.

Although the idea of redistricting had originally been his, Dionisije had intended to retain control of all three bishops by elevating himself to the office of metropolite. He refused to recognize the Synod's proposed reorganization, attributing it to Communist efforts to destroy the free church by dividing it, using the Belgrade patriarch as a puppet. As a result of his refusal to comply, Dionisije was deposed as bishop in July 1963 and divested in March of the following year.

*Bishop Dionisije performs the service for the 50th anniversary of St. Sava Serbian Orthodox Church at Libertyville, Illinois.*

While the Synod proceeded with its reorganization plan, Dionisije rallied supporters among clergy and community, presenting his struggle with Belgrade as a struggle against domination of the free church by Communist Yugoslavia and its officially atheist government. Moved by loyalty to Dionisije and a suspicion of Yugoslavia, about one-third of the parishes in the North American Diocese sided with Dionisije's cause. Many parishes were split apart by the issue, and a number of new churches formed to serve the minority factions. In New York, for example, the majority of the members of St. Sava Church on 21st Street sided with Dionisije's autonomy faction, and the portion of the congregation who were in opposition left the church. To this day, they hold separate services in a chapel within the Cathedral of St. John the Divine. The battle over Dionisije raged for years, and in some communities it even led to physical violence. By 1976, the issue had reached as far as the U.S. Supreme Court. Although the court ruled against Dionisije and his followers, this legal decision did little to lessen the continued emotional impact of the schism on Serbian Americans. Dionisije's charged language expresses the continued bitterness of the controversy and draws a parallel between his struggle and that of the Serbian nation:

> We will not hand over to our enemies Libertyville, but rather we will defend it, if necessary, with our blood, as every foot of Serbian land was defended in the struggle for liberty.

To some degree, the religious division within the Serbian-American community reflects long-standing tensions between different generations of Serbian immigrants, particularly between the old settlers and the newcomers. Many newcomers, especially former Yugoslav army officers, were bitterly disappointed at their reduced status in the United States. In Bishop Dionisije, they found a voice for their personal and professional discontent as well as for their political beliefs in regard to Yugoslavia. The newcomers focus on the need to defend the purity of Serbian customs against what they see as the Communist threat to their culture.

The old settlers, whose time in America predates the Communist regime in the homeland, tend to be more concerned with Serbian-American affairs than Yugoslav politics. Most support the unity faction, viewing a break with the mother church as a violation of canonical law. They feel that the primary role of the church is to teach Orthodox truths and organize Serbs into a cohesive spiritual community, whereas the newcomers, with their international perspective, tend to favor the autonomy faction, led by Dionisije.

Those advocating unity with the Belgrade patriarch have accused the Dionisije faction, called the Free Church in America, of the heresy of dividing a national church 750 years old. In turn, the Free Church faction labels their opponents Communist sympathizers. To add to the confusion, many Serbs have straddled the two factions, maintaining ties with "the other side." Though conflicting feelings continue to tear at the fabric of the Serbian community, moves toward reconciliation have recently been made. Ultimately, in spite of internal dissension, the church continues to function as a source of unity for the Serbs.

The church's significance to the Serbian-American community extends far beyond the domain of religion. A typical neighborhood church's calendar is filled with commitments to social and service organizations, from folk dance and music clubs to choral societies and the Circle of Serbian Sisters (a ladies' auxiliary). Local chapters of these organizations link churchgoers to a national network. Many churches have athletic leagues as well and hold weekly get-togethers at which Serbs gather for music, conversation, and drink. In the summertime, the *Srbobran* runs pages of notices for church-sponsored picnics, concerts, and festivals.

Orthodoxy also influences the Serbian-American identity in other, more private ways. The first of these is *kumstvo*, or godparenthood. Parents choose a *kum* or *kuma* (a male or female godparent) for their child shortly after its birth. This honored person may then select a name that he or she will bestow upon the child at its baptism. Beyond this, the kum or kuma is responsible for ensuring the moral and material well-being of the child. The concept of kumstvo extends to Serbian ceremonies and organizations, when a kum or kuma is designated to play the role of honorary chairperson.

Of even greater significance is the celebration of a family's religious anniversary, known as *krsna slava*. Slava is held once a year to commemorate the conversion of the family's ancestors to Christianity back in

*A minister consecrates the ground on the building site of St. Nicholas Serbian Orthodox Church in Hamilton, Ontario, in 1967. The Orthodox church has continued to exert a strong influence on Serbian Americans in recent decades.*

the 9th or 10th century. The family celebrates with a feast of typical Serbian fare, featuring dishes, such as boiled wheat, that link the observance back to pre-Christian harvest rituals. The essential element in the feast is the *kolach*, a ritual loaf of bread baked especially for slava and usually decorated with dough replicas of birds or wheat and symbols of the cross and the "Four S's." During the slava feast a priest will visit the home and conduct a ritual in which the kolach is raised three times, to symbolize the Holy Trinity. Then the priest or head of the family cuts a cross in the bottom of the loaf into which he pours wine symbolizing the blood of Christ.

Candles and incense help create a sacred atmosphere. The sound of friendly chatter and laughter fills the room as the family shares its food and drink with its guests. All have gathered to celebrate the family's membership in a tradition that stretches back 1,000 years to the conversion of the Slavs. Slava celebrations link family members scattered across the continent and the globe to a common heritage in an Orthodox Serbia. Without this ceremony, there would be no Serbian Orthodoxy, and without its Orthodox heritage, the identity of the Serbian people would cease to exist. Slava, then, is the key to the "unity that saves the Serbs."

South Slav settlers in Utah pose with their instruments near the turn of the century. Music has always been a unifying element in the Serbian-American community.

# HE WHO SINGS THINKS NO EVIL

During the centuries that the Ottoman Empire ruled over Serbia, wandering minstrels traveled from village to village playing a simple bowed instrument called the *gusla*. These musicians, or *guslari*, helped to unify a scattered and conquered people by bringing news from town to town and keeping alive the ancient songs of the Serbs. The words of their ballads preserved the legends of Serbian heroes and the history of the Serbian people.

Though the gusla itself is rarely played among Serbian immigrants in America, musicians continue to play a crucial role in uniting the community. Church holidays, such private occasions as an anniversary or slava, and such community events as SNF sports tournaments, are all celebrated to the accompaniment of Serbian music.

Serbian-American music is often played by tamburitza orchestras. Tamburitzas are a family of long-necked lutes, something like stretched mandolins, that immigrants from the Austro-Hungarian territories, especially Croatia, brought with them to North America. Serbs share their love of tamburitza music with the Croatians; the repertoire, styles, and even the nationalities of performing ensembles are mixed. What counts is the musician's skill, not his or her country of origin.

*A trio of Serbian musicians pose in a rural setting with violin, bass, and* tamburitza.

Tamburitza musicians are hired, and tipped well if successful, because they create a familiar and exciting atmosphere for listening and dancing. Sometimes they play their songs while standing near the bar or a listener's table. One member of the audience will often request a particular tune, which then becomes "his song." He or she gestures appreciatively, sings along, and generally leads the audience's response. When the song is over, he tips the player with a dramatic flourish, by sticking money in the musician's instrument or pocket, or even on his forehead. Some of these songs portray a love of life, music, and pleasure; others harken back to Yugoslavia, evoking customs and places of the old country.

Some of the tunes in the tamburitza repertoire are intended solely for dancing. The characteristic dance of Serbian Americans is the *kolo*. Although its name means circle, the most common kolo is actually performed in a line, with the dancers holding each other's belt or holding hands. Men and women, teenage girls in blue jeans and heels, and grandmothers in floral print dresses all join together in the execution of the simple but lively steps. Larger parties may have several orchestras playing, one for each of the lines.

Despite its long history and the recent popularity of more modern instruments, tamburitza music is still thriving in the United States. Any doubter need only visit the annual Tamburitza Extravaganza, where more than 20 bands from around the country perform for 3 days. Any issue of the *Srborbran*, with its list of five or six upcoming picnics and celebrations at which orchestras will play, might also convince the skeptic. There is even a Tamburitza Hall of Fame in St. Louis, Missouri, as well as four or five active manufacturers of tamburitza instruments in the United States.

The continued vitality of this music in America today owes much to the efforts of early teachers of the art of tamburitza, such as George Kachar, who brought the music from his homeland to a small mining town in Colorado. There, during the 1920s, he trained a class of pupils in technique and repertoire. Among his students were four gifted brothers named Popovich: Eli, Adam, Teddy, and Marko. They learned their lessons

*The Popovich Brothers and George Kachar, their music teacher, in the 1920s. From left to right are Marko, Eli, Adam, and Ted Popovich and George Kachar.*

well and have spent more than 60 years performing tamburitza music, first by traveling among the widely scattered Yugoslav mining communities of the West; later, as residents of South Chicago, where they appeared regularly in clubs, made recordings, and taught others. The Popovich Brothers have played in the White House and represented Yugoslav Americans in the "Salute to Immigrant Cultures" organized by the Ethnic Folk Arts Center of New York for the Statue of Liberty celebrations in 1986. Other great teachers and performers have included Frank and Marty Kapugi, Tillie Klaich, and the Crlenica Brothers. Numerous books and methods have been written to instruct young players, and specialty labels preserve the music on record.

The most important force behind the recruiting and training of young tamburitza musicians has undoubtedly been the Duquesne University Tamburitzans. Through their institute for folklore, their scholarships for promising students, and their well-organized system of junior tamburitzan organizations, the influence of the "Tammies" has spread to communities across the country. Their director, Walter Kolar, passes on a regard for musical technique, authentic styling, and traditional repertoire, which the Tammies themselves

The Serbian folksinger Edo Lubich arrived in America from Yugoslavia in 1939. His name soon became a household word to Serbian Americans who loved his songs and music from the Old World.

reinforce through the excellence of their own performances. As a result, the tradition remains very much alive among young Yugoslav Americans today.

*Tamburashi*, as the musicians who play this music are known, must be fiercely devoted to their craft. Because they tend to perform their music late at night and in widely scattered locations, a tamburash often has to sacrifice not only sleep but personal and professional relations. Most players work at other jobs, but many do not rise to the professional levels that they would otherwise reach because of the time they give to their music. Their dedication also often strains marriages and friendships.

Still, their devotion is intense; as one Steelton musician expressed it, "My wife doesn't understand why I go out to play at midnight, but the love of the tambura is powerful." Another tamburash, whose hand was damaged in an industrial accident, smashed his instrument in rage, but he later learned to play all of his favorite tunes on the piano.

Since World War II new musical styles have become popular in Serbian-American communities. The postwar immigrants play a distinctively "Serbian" style, often on amplified modern instruments, especially accordions, keyboards, and drums. The repertoire of these bands changes rapidly to keep up with trends in Serbia, where this form of "folk music" (*narodna muzika*) constitutes a regular industry. Much like the Nashville sound, this newly composed folk music combines traditional-sounding melodies and styles with state-of-the-art instrumentation, sophisticated arrangements, and modern production techniques.

Such bands feature a singer, usually a woman, who combines vocal virtuosity with the sex appeal of a rock star. This music, often performed by visiting artists from Yugoslavia, is very popular among the most recent waves of immigrants, who go to hear it in restaurants and *kafanas* (coffeehouses). Many of the older immigrants and their descendants dislike these new groups, which they refer to as "boom-boom bands." Whatever style they prefer, Serbs in America are connected to their homeland through their music.

Choral music is another very important part of the musical life of Serbs in North America. The central organization of choral music is the Serbian Singing Federation of the USA and Canada (SSF), which sponsors a full calendar of concerts each year across the continent. The founder of the SSF, Vladimir (Vlako) Lugonja, had first sung in the Branko Radicevich Choir of Chicago, which is still among the country's most active, and had also organized choirs in Detroit. He conceived of the idea to form a federation of choirs just after the stock market crash of 1929 and succeeded in doing so, though initially with only five choirs, in 1931. Singing helped the Serbs fight the gloom of the Great Depression of the 1930s. Lugonja then worked for many decades to increase the size of the organization as well as the extent of its repertoire. He toured Yugoslavia in 1937 and brought back a vast quantity of choral music. By World War II, the membership of the SSF had grown to 30 choirs. The annual convention of the SSF continues to draw singers from all over the world, and a number of its choirs have gone on tour in the United States and in Europe, including Yugoslavia.

The SSF has a motto that expresses well the role played by music and dance among Serbian Americans: *Ko Peva, Zlo Ne Misli* (He Who Sings Thinks No Evil.) Music remains a joyful expression of Serbian identity and community, its familiar rhythms and lyrics reason enough to draw together in celebration.

*Today's Serbian bands often update the sound of the homeland through the use of electric guitars, accordions, and heavy amplification.*

# STANDING OUT
# FROM THE CROWD

The history of Serbian immigration is an on-going story of one people's contribution to North American society. As each successive wave has arrived, unknown thousands have begun to serve this country through their skills and hard work. Serbian religious and social institutions have done more than offer support to their members; they have added a new vitality to the American landscape. Serbian music and folklore continue to enrich American society and add welcome diversity to American culture. The anonymous contributions of the unsung steelworker and the junior tamburitzan playing his first kolo have been in their way as great as the contributions of Serbian Americans who have distinguished themselves from the crowd.

Serbs can also look proudly at the accomplishments of a number of their people who have risen to prominent positions in science, sports, and the arts. Since most Serbs came to the New World without wealth or education, such successes are a particular tribute to the unusual talent and determination of these individuals.

## Inventors

Michael Pupin's hardship did not end with the discomfort of his passage in 1874 and his first disappointing slice of prune pie as a 15-year-old greenhorn in Battery Park. In the years following his arrival in America, he worked as a farmhand, a factory worker, a wagon painter, and a day laborer, until one day he was smitten by a vision of greatness.

By his own account, while eating a loaf of bread on the campus of Princeton University, where he had happened to wander after leaving one of his farm jobs, he had a sudden revelation: He was filled with an intense awareness of the greatness all around him and the desire to achieve that lay dormant within him. He experienced a similar moment at the Cooper Union Institute in New York, where he was a regular user of its technical library. His vision of a world in which dreams could become a reality inspired him to work unwaveringly to gain college admission while simultaneously working his way up in a cracker factory.

Pupin was tutored by an eccentric former scientist named Biharz, who urged him to learn classical languages and literature and advised him to enter Adelphi Academy to prepare for college. Pupin's diligence paid off in 1879, when he won a full scholarship to Columbia University after astounding the professors with his perfect recitation of Homer and Cicero in their original Greek and Latin forms.

After continuing his studies in England and Germany, Pupin returned to Columbia University in 1889 as an instructor of mathematical physics. Over the next decade he devised three crucial inventions: the electrical tuner used in radios, a process for greatly reducing X-ray exposures, and, most significantly, a patented "high inductance wave conductor" that used coils to help send telephone signals over long stretches of wire. He remained a professor at Columbia for most of his life, where the physics building bears his name.

Pupin distinguished himself outside the scientific world as well. He received a Pulitzer Prize for his autobiography, *From Immigrant to Inventor*, which Scribners published in 1924. The book is filled with loving references to his home village, and in discussing his inventions, Pupin gave less credit to his academic training than to his childhood lessons with village shepherds. From them he learned the basics of a very practical form of physics: how to send signals through the ground using knives, how to use the stars as clock and compass, and how to use the sound of the village church bell to determine wind direction. Pupin, who was credited with adding the word "tuner" to the English language, explains its origins in Serbian folklore:

> Few things excited my interest more than the operation of the Serbian bagpiper as he forced the air from his bellows and made it sing by regulating its passage through the pipes. The operations which the bagpiper called adjustment and tuning of the bagpipes commanded my closest attention. I never dreamed that a score of years later I should do a similar operation with an electrical circuit. I called it "electrical tuning," a term which has been generally accepted in wireless telegraphy. But nobody knows that the operation as well as the name was first suggested to me by the Serbian bagpiper some twenty years before I made the invention in 1892.

Pupin's love for his Serbian homeland inspired him to political action on its behalf. He became one of the founders and the first president of the SND, organized in New York in 1914 to aid a homeland beset by war. After the war, in 1919, he also served as a member of the American delegation to the Paris Peace Conference. When he died, in 1935, Pupin left behind a rich and varied legacy of scientific, literary, and political achievement.

Nikola Tesla received 112 U.S. patents for his discoveries. Like Thomas Edison, his onetime employer and later rival, Tesla was a pioneer in the transmission of electric power. His first important discovery was what he called the rotary magnetic field, an arrangement of electromagnetic units that used alternating

*Michael Pupin was undaunted by his early struggles as a greenhorn in the streets of New York. By the end of the 19th century, his intellectual curiosity and brilliance had led him to the forefront of the scientific world.*

*Scientist Nikola Tesla in 1914 at age 58. His brilliant contemporary Thomas Edison called the visionary Tesla a ''poet of science.''*

current (AC) to turn a metal bar. Although AC had been used before for lighting, Tesla found a way to connect this current to a motor, a development that ultimately determined the nature of the power systems used in the United States and throughout the world.

In a lifetime of experimentation following this early discovery, Tesla's genius applied itself in a variety of ways: He devised many of the components still used in radio, explored an early form of robotics and remote control, shook the ground and shattered huge objects with his experiments in resonance, and even talked of developing a death ray and an electronic defense shield to be used in space. At the peak of his career, Tesla commanded the admiration of the world; at its depths he dug ditches and bore his frustrations alone.

Tesla was born in 1856 to Serbian parents in the town of Smiljan, in Croatia. In later years he would affirm his dual origins by describing his homeland as Croatia and his nationality as Serbian. His father and maternal grandfather were Orthodox priests, and Nikola was expected to follow suit, but at a young age Tesla began to see things no one else did. Some of these visions and flights of fancy presaged his later genius: At four years old, experimenting with human flight, he hyperventilated on the roof of a barn and then jumped, using the family umbrella as a parachute—with predictable results. At five, he devised a motor with June bugs as its power source, and at seven, he saved the day at a picnic in the town of Gospic, his family's new home, by diving into the river to straighten out a kink that was preventing the town's new fire-fighting equipment from working.

At other times, Tesla's visions were more troublesome. He literally saw things that were not there; objects, situations, blackboards filled with equations, all appeared before his eyes with the clarity of reality. This by-product of Tesla's high-strung genius would plague him throughout his life.

Tesla's childhood was characterized by illness—he contracted both malaria and cholera—and academic achievement. By the time he reached age 19, Tesla had managed to convince his father to acquiesce to his scientific ambitions, and he was sent to the Polytechnical

School in Gratz. There Tesla threw himself into his studies with an alarming intensity, often sleeping no more than two or three hours per night. Extremist, sometimes destructive behavior—gambling binges temporarily derailed his later studies—would remain a lifelong characteristic.

A professor who ridiculed Tesla's ideas concerning an AC motor inadvertently sparked the driven young man to focus all his previously undirected intellectual energy on this question alone, whose solution he first scratched out in the dirt of a Budapest park while strolling with a friend.

After completing his education and working for several years for the European branches of a number of American companies, including Edison's, Tesla decided to come to America. On his way to the boat, he was robbed of his money, baggage, and ticket and was allowed to board only because he had used his photographic memory to record his exact ticket number. Consequently, Tesla arrived in even direr economic straits than most immigrants, with only four cents in his pocket, but he did possess a considerable wealth of ideas, imagination, and experience.

Tesla worked briefly for Edison, who called him "a poet of science," but the two men parted ways after arguments about money and disagreements about the relative merits of AC and direct current (DC). Edison championed the latter, so that when Tesla's work caught the attention of Edison's business rival George Westinghouse, the battle of the currents was joined.

During the barrage of propaganda that ensued, Edison went so far as to encourage the use of AC for the electric chair at New York's Auburn prison so as to label it the dangerous "executioner's current." But in the end, Westinghouse's system, based on Tesla's inventions, won out.

For much of the 1890s, Tesla's work made him an international sensation. He had his own exhibit at the Columbia Exposition of 1893 in Chicago, where, elegantly dressed in top hat and tails, he passed enormous voltages through his body to illuminate bulbs and other contrivances. He often provided equally dramatic shows for his many dinner guests, including the likes of Mark Twain, the great novelist and satirist. Among the many society ladies who adored him was Anne Morgan, the handsome daughter of the wealthy banker and financier J. P. Morgan. She reportedly fell in love with the eccentric inventor but made the mistake of wearing pearl earrings to their first private meeting. Pearls and earrings were among Tesla's many phobias, which also included dirty linen and certain foods. In any case, he was adamantly opposed to marriage, believing that no great invention had ever been produced by a married man. He lived for many years in unencumbered bachelorhood at the Waldorf-Astoria Hotel in Manhattan, where, though surrounded by society, he remained at heart a solitary man impassioned by his own creative forces.

As Tesla himself explained, "I do not think there is any thrill that can go through the human heart like that felt by the inventor as he sees some creation of the brain unfolding to success. . . . Such emotions make a man forget food, sleep, friends, love, everything."

Tesla paid a high price for his genius. Because his inventions were so ahead of their time, they were often not of immediate practical use and earned him little or no money, forcing Tesla, in later life, to scrounge for funds to continue his work. As he grew older, Tesla also began to succumb more frequently to the bouts of nervous sensitivity that had haunted him since childhood. He would only stay in a hotel room whose number was divisible by three, and he grew so sensitive to sound that he resorted to padding his bedposts to absorb vibrations, the slightest of which caused him great discomfort. As an old man, he took to spending hours alone in New York's Bryant Park feeding the pigeons. He died in 1943, in self-imposed seclusion, at the age of 86.

Tesla is now a national hero in Yugoslavia, where a museum has been erected in his honor. The International Tesla Society continues to investigate and publicize the importance of his discoveries. In 1956, the centennial of his birth, the International Electrotechnical Commission gave his name to a standard

*Tesla calmly takes notes in his Colorado Springs laboratory while his "Tesla coil" sends several million volts of electricity cascading into the air around him.*

electrical unit. In 1976 a statue of Tesla was unveiled on the Goat Island power station at Niagara Falls in homage to his uncanny brilliance.

## The Performing Arts

Two Serbian-American performers in the world of theater and film stand out from all others. The first, Karl Malden, was born in 1914 in Chicago to Petar and Sebera Sekulovich. Though christened with the authentic Serbian name of Mladen Sekulovich, he took his stage name very early in his career. Malden's father had been an actor in Europe, but in America, like most old-settler immigrants, he was forced to take work as an unskilled laborer and eventually as a milkman in Gary, Indiana, where the family moved when Karl was young.

Malden first developed an interest in acting while at Arkansas State Teachers College, which he attended on a basketball scholarship. When his basketball coach

*A publicity still taken of actor Karl Malden shortly after he won the 1951 Academy Award for Best Supporting Actor for his portrayal of Mitch, the shy suitor of Blanche DuBois in the film version of Tennessee Williams's* Streetcar Named Desire.

told Malden to choose between the sport and appearing in a student production, Malden left school. He spent the next few years earning a living as a semipro basketball player and, like many a Serbian American before him, by working in a steel mill. A scholarship to the Goodman Theatre Dramatic School in Chicago freed him from the mill, and after three years of study there Malden made his way to New York City in 1938.

Malden's first significant role was in Clifford Odets's play *Golden Boy*. Through this experience he met the director Elia Kazan, who would later cast him in his most celebrated roles.

After compiling a long list of solid credits, Malden scored his first big hit in Arthur Miller's *All My Sons*, directed by Kazan. The New York Drama Critics voted it the best play of 1946–47. This critical praise was followed by national recognition for his performance in Tennessee Williams's Pulitzer Prize–winning *Streetcar Named Desire*, directed by Kazan, which played on Broadway in 1947–48. In 1951, Malden received an Oscar for his performance in the movie version, also directed by Kazan. He received a second Oscar nomination for his portrayal of the courageous priest in *On the Waterfront* in 1954. In recent years he has become a familiar sight on television, appearing as the lead detective in the television series "The Streets of San Francisco" and as the concerned but severe figure warning Americans not to leave home without American Express travelers' checks.

Malden succeeded as an actor without the glamorous good looks that most people assume a star needs. He comes across on stage and screen as an endearing, if somewhat ungainly, character whose earnest intensity has the ring of conviction. In 1987 he paid tribute to his Serbian-American roots on the "Larry King Live" television show, where he reminisced about his father, who had acted and sung at the Serbian church in Gary and served as one of the founders of the SSF.

In more recent years another actor of Serbian descent, John Malkovich, has captured the attention of the American people. Malden and Malkovich have a surprising amount in common aside from their similar heritage. Both of them grew up in the Midwest and built their careers by working over a number of years with a small core of close friends. Each moved into movie work after first establishing himself on the Broadway stage.

Like Malden, Malkovich has a reputation for violating the accepted norms of how a star should act and look. He is prematurely balding, pigeon-toed, and soft-spoken to the point of inaudibility. Sometimes compared to Marlon Brando, James Dean, Robert De Niro, or Jack Nicholson, Malkovich projects a bruised, urgent thoughtfulness where the potential for a violent outburst seems held in check just below the surface.

Malkovich grew up in the small town of Benton, Illinois. He began to act while a student at East Illinois State University. In 1976, he and a group of nine friends founded the Steppenwolf Theater Company in Chicago. The close-knit group remained intact for 10 years, providing Chicago with first-rate productions of both classical and contemporary drama. Malkovich not only acted in the company but also directed and designed sets and costumes. Like Malden in Gary a generation before, he found ways to pay the bills, such as driving a school bus and selling office supplies.

*The brooding intensity that John Malkovich brings to his stage and screen portrayals has made him one of the most successful and praised American actors of the 1980s.*

For six years, Malkovich worked as an ensemble actor, drawing no more recognition than the other members of Steppenwolf. He began to emerge as a star with the role of Lee in Sam Shepard's *True West*, for which he won the Joseph Jefferson Award in 1982. The production moved to New York with great success. Malkovich won an Obie for his performance, and the production was filmed for a broadcast on Public Television.

Things moved quickly from that point. After winning rave reviews and popular acclaim for his understated, pensive Biff in *Death of a Salesman*, starring Dustin Hoffman, Malkovich went on to perform in Lanford Wilson's play *Burn This* and to direct Wilson's *Balm in Gilead* at the Circle Repertory Theater in New York. He has since demonstrated his wide range as an actor in a variety of films to date, including *Making Mr. Right*, *Places in the Heart* (for which he won an Oscar nomination), *The Killing Fields, Eleni*, and most recently, the highly successful *Dangerous Liaisons*. In a 1984 *Esquire* article, David Blum wrote, "At thirty years old, Malkovich is one of the top American stage actors of his generation."

## The Frontier of Possibility

When acting in *Eleni*, Malkovich was reading the words of another Serbian American, the screenwriter Steven Tesich. This award-winning dramatist was born in Titovo Užice, Serbia, in 1942 and moved to Gary, Indiana, with his family at the age of 14. After receiving a B.A. from Indiana University and an M.A. from Columbia, where he studied Russian literature, Tesich went to work as a free-lance writer and won an Oscar for the screenplay of his first movie, *Breaking Away*, which describes coming of age in the industrial Midwest. His other screen credits include *Eyewitness; Four Friends*, which explores the themes of sorting out love and identity in an ethnic industrial neighborhood in the 1960s, on the eve of the Vietnam era; *The World According to Garp;* and *Eleni*, a dramatization of reporter Nicholas Gage's encounters with communism.

Tesich's immigrant background has clearly influenced his writing. Much of his work explores the individual's search for identity and the possibility of finding a place in American society. He grew up with a distrust of communism, which may have led him to accept the *Eleni* assignment, as well as a willfully naive idealism and a desire for community. The idealistic and revolutionary spirit of the 1960s was a powerful inspiration because it harkened back to his childhood vision of America as a place where wrongs could be righted. In a 1982 *New York Times Magazine* article, Tesich recalled his early efforts at fiction, which consisted of storytelling in the war-torn village of Titovo Užice:

> I spent a lot of time making up stories for my friends, for the old men. There were no young men—the war had taken care of them. I'd make up stories about my father who was missing.

Everyone's father was missing. So my stories would always be about going to America and finding my Papa.

Tesich was reunited with his father in the United States after 14 years of separation. Because of his father's training as a machinist, the family ended up in the industrial heartland rather than in the American West that the young Tesich had seen in the John Wayne movies shown in Serbia. In spite of this discrepancy between life and the silver screen, Tesich "really believed he had found another frontier, the frontier of possibility." Through his work, Tesich was able to transform the hope and the pain of his own experience as a Serbian immigrant into a description of the universal human experience.

## Showtime

Serbian organizations place a great deal of emphasis on athletics, and many Serbs have become players, coaches, and managers of professional American teams. One of the best-known basketball players in the history of the game, Pete Maravich, was of Serbian ancestry.

Maravich's dedication to the game began at a young age. His father, Press, was a basketball coach who instilled in his promising son the need for discipline and invented an endless variety of imaginative ball-handling drills, such as dribbling in theater aisles, out the window of a moving car, and blindfolded. These early years of intense father-and-son workouts paid off in ball-handling flair and expertise that none could match.

Maravich began playing for his father's squad at Louisiana State University in 1966; he left 4 years later with the moniker "Pistol Pete," having averaged a record 44.2 points per game. During his college years he also refined his unparalleled skill as a master court showman, thrilling crowds with his dazzling ball handling and trick shots, a unique repertoire of basketball legerdemain he called showtime. By graduation, Maravich had become a superstar, and he signed a contract with the Atlanta Hawks for $1.5 million, one of the largest sums ever given to a rookie. Scores of young ballplayers around the country idolized and emulated him, even adopting his trademark floppy gray sweat socks.

Maravich played professionally from 1970 to 1980. Although he averaged a sterling 24.2 points per game over the course of his career, led the league in scoring in 1976–77, made several All-Star teams, and always remained a crowd favorite, his career was unfulfilling. His reputation and salary created extremely high expectations and sometimes alienated his teammates. While none denied his remarkable talent, critics charged that Maravich was not a team player and was more interested in showtime than in winning games. In his defense, it must be said that Maravich spent the bulk of his career with weak teams for which he was the major drawing card; it is doubtful that those franchises wished him to rein in his game. After his retirement at the young age of 31, Maravich cited his failure to play on a championship squad as his biggest disappointment.

Maravich endured hard times after leaving the game. Not only had he not reached his potential as a professional, but he was now faced with the unresolved issues in his personal life that may have played a part in his early retirement. His mother had died from alcoholism, and Maravich had struggled with a drinking problem throughout his professional career. In an effort toward self-improvement, Maravich had become a vegetarian in 1976, and after leaving the pros, his need to find inner peace and self-understanding intensified. After a long spiritual search, he became a born-again Christian. In the last years of his life, he ran the Pistol Pete All-Star Camp at Clearwater Christian College in Florida, produced a series of training videos, and made public appearances to speak about sports and family values. His autobiography, *Heir to a Dream*, was published in 1987. One year later, while playing an exhibition game in California, Maravich suffered a heart attack and died. He will long be remembered for his mastery of the game, his charismatic on-court presence, and his triumphant struggle to find personal fulfillment.

*Pete Maravich meets the press shortly after signing a contract with the Boston Celtics in 1980. The Celtics are traditionally one of professional basketball's most successful franchises, but Maravich's dream of a championship continued to elude him.*

*Thousands of Serbians congregated at Kosovo on June 28, 1989, to celebrate the 600th anniversary of the battle there.*

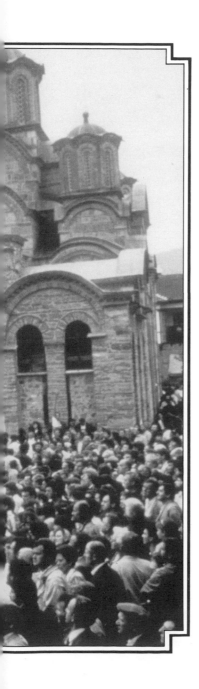

# NO ONE HAS WHAT
# THE SERB HAS

The Fourth of July in the United States and the First of July in Canada are celebrated as Independence Day in those countries, and both nations celebrate their military triumphs on Armistice Day, November 11. In significant contrast, Serbians commemorate the day of their national defeat rather than of their independence. Every year on June 28, *Vidovdan* marks the fall of Serbian forces to the invading Ottoman Turks at the Battle of Kosovo in 1389. On that day, the heroism and death of Czar Lazar is commemorated in the form of epics sung by the guslari and in sketches of the battle that appear on the front page of the *Srbobran*.

The ambivalence inherent in this celebration typifies the Serbians' twofold sense of themselves: They are both proud of their culture and customs and determined to survive amid the adversity that has threatened their identity for as long as they have existed as a people. It might seem strange that the Serbs commemorate a defeat, but what is really being celebrated are the values that enable them to withstand adversity. The slogan Only Unity Will Save the Serbs expresses the precautionary position they maintain in readiness for the inevitability of attack. Serbs, both in their homeland and in America, have had to learn to fight to survive as a people.

The greatest adversity facing the Serbian-American identity today may well be the passage of time itself. Many of the old settlers are gone now, having taken with them the memories of the first great surge of Serbian immigration. While the Četniks and political refugees of World War II retain their organizations and publications, their political agenda seems increasingly unlikely to be achieved. Many of the recent arrivals from Yugoslavia feel little or no connection to the older communities, whose members continue to feel the anguish caused by the split in the Serbian Orthodox church.

Furthermore, several powerful forces threaten the cohesion of Serbian communities as America's economic base shifts from heavy industry to services. Like their ancestors, young Serbs seeking opportunity tend to venture to new regions in search of employment in communities that are less insular and more stable than their own. Better educated than their forebears, second-and third-generation Serbian Americans are now able to choose professional careers. That these offspring should avail themselves of opportunities unavailable to their parents and grandparents is the mixed blessing resulting from their predecessors' successful devotion to their working-class livelihoods.

Serbs face these threats to their ethnic identity with the same courage that has enabled them to overcome so many obstacles, aided by a solid network of support. Their identity is firmly anchored in the church and the many organizations it sponsors as well as in the SNF, which unifies Serbs through its tournaments and festivals, and through the *Srbobran*, which acts like a modern-day guslar connecting scattered individuals and remote communities with their common heritage. In 1987, the SNF published an updated edition of the Serbian primer to encourage a new generation of Serbian Americans to learn the language of their ancestors. Institutions like slava and kumstvo further solidify the Serbs' sense of themselves.

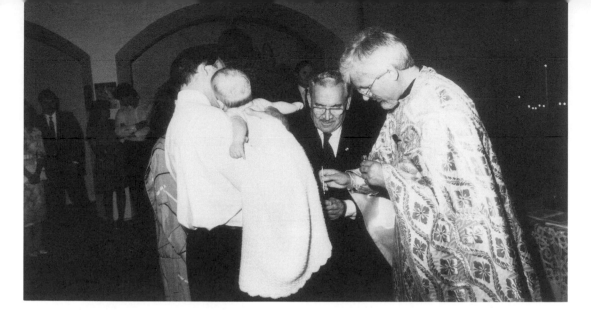

Over the last two decades, a greater ethnic consciousness has developed among most immigrant groups, including the Serbians. As Yugoslavia becomes a more open society and people and news travel freely back and forth across the Atlantic, Serbs in North America are now able to learn more about their roots.

Being Serbian is not only a solemn duty; it is a pleasure. Young Serbs in North America can look to role models like Michael Pupin, Nikola Tesla, and John Malkovich for inspiration.

Singing, dancing, socializing with friends, and celebrating holidays—all these things make Serbian-American identity as much a joy as an obligation. Ask the teenager from Cleveland who brings his school friends home to share in the family's slava celebration. Ask the team that won this year's SNF basketball tournament or the 15 year old who gives up his Saturdays to learn to play the tamburitza.

As long as Serbian Americans have their church, their music, and their folklore, they will retain their essential identity, no matter what other changes affect the community. All North Americans benefit from their unique contribution to life here. As the Serbian song says, "*Niko nema sta srbin imade*" ("No one has what a Serb has"). That has remained true into the fourth and fifth generation, and it promises to remain so in the years to come.

*A christening at the Christ Resurrection Serbian Orthodox Church in Chicago. The success of Serbian Americans in maintaining tradition and their ethnic identity gives reason for optimism concerning the future cohesiveness of the Serbian-American community.*

# FURTHER READING

Auty, Phyllis. *Yugoslavia.* New York: Walker and Co., 1965.

Dedijer, Vladimir, et al. *History of Yugoslavia.* New York: McGraw-Hill, 1974.

Eterovich, Adam S. *Yugoslav Survey of California, Nevada, Arizona, and the South, 1830–1900.* San Francisco: R & E Research Associates, 1971.

———. *Yugoslavs in Nevada, 1858–1900.* San Francisco: R & E Research Associates, 1973.

Hunt, Inez, and Wanetta Draper. *Lightning in His Hand: The Life Story of Nikola Tesla.* Denver: Sage Books, 1964.

Padgett, Deborah. "Settlers and Sojourners: A Study of Serbian Adaption in Milwaukee, Wisconsin." Ph.D. diss., University of Wisconsin, 1979.

Petrovich, Michael Boro. *A History of Modern Serbia: 1804–1918.* 2 vols. New York: Harcourt Brace Jovanovich, 1976.

Popescu, Julian. *Let's Visit Yugoslavia.* London: Burke Publishing Co. Ltd., 1984.

Pupin, Michael. *From Immigrant to Inventor.* New York: Scribners, 1924.

Singleton, Fred. *A Short History of the Yugoslav Peoples.* New York: Cambridge University Press, 1985.

Vrga, Djuro J. *Changes and Socio-Religious Conflict in an Ethnic Minority Group: The Serbian Orthodox Church in America.* San Francisco: R & E Research Associates, 1975.

# INDEX

# PICTURE CREDITS

JEROME KISSLINGER received an M.A. in Russian studies from Columbia University. He now teaches English at the Horace Mann School in New York City and works as a free-lance writer. He maintains close ties to the Serbian community and performs music for Serbians both in the United States and in Yugoslavia.

DANIEL PATRICK MOYNIHAN is the senior United States senator from New York. He is also the only person in American history to serve in the cabinets or subcabinets of four successive presidents—Kennedy, Johnson, Nixon, and Ford. Formerly a professor of government at Harvard University, he has written and edited many books, including *Beyond the Melting Pot, Ethnicity: Theory and Experience* (both with Nathan Glazer), *Loyalties,* and *Family and Nation.*